HAMILTON'S CURSE

ALSO BY THOMAS J. DiLORENZO

LINCOLN UNMASKED
What You're Not Supposed to Know About Dishonest Abe

HOW CAPITALISM SAVED AMERICA
The Untold History of Our Country, from the Pilgrims to the Present

THE REAL LINCOLN
*A New Look at Abraham Lincoln, His Agenda,
and an Unnecessary War*

HAMILTON'S
CURSE

How Jefferson's Archenemy

Betrayed the American Revolution —

and What It Means for Americans Today

THOMAS J. DiLORENZO

THREE RIVERS PRESS

NEW YORK

Copyright © 2008 by Thomas J. DiLorenzo

Published in the United States by Three Rivers Press, an imprint of the
Crown Publishing Group, a division of
Random House, Inc., New York.
www.crownpublishing.com

Three Rivers Press and the Tugboat design are registered trademarks of
Random House, Inc.

Originally published in hardcover in the United States by Crown Forum, an imprint of the
Crown Publishing Group, a division of Random House, Inc., New York, in 2008.

Library of Congress Cataloging-in-Publication Data
DiLorenzo, Thomas J.
Hamilton's curse : how Jefferson's archenemy betrayed the
American revolution—and what it means for Americans today /
Thomas J. DiLorenzo.—1st ed.
p. cm.
Includes bibliographical references and index.
1. Hamilton, Alexander, 1757–1804—Political and social views.
2. Hamilton, Alexander, 1757–1804—Influence.   3. United States—Politics and
government—Philosophy.   4. Political culture—United States.   I. Title.

E302.H2D55 2008
973.4092—dc22
[B]
2008017535

ISBN 978-0-307-38285-6

Design by Leonard W. Henderson

First Paperback Edition

Dedicated to the memory of

Professor Murray N. Rothbard,

a brilliant scholar and tireless defender of the free society.

CONTENTS

INTRODUCTION

The Real Hamilton

*[T]he power to raise money is plenary and indefinite
[in the Constitution]. . . . The terms general Welfare
were doubtless intended to signify more than was
expressed.*

—ALEXANDER HAMILTON,
REPORT ON MANUFACTURES

*Implied powers are to be considered as delegated
equally [to the federal government] with express ones.*
—ALEXANDER HAMILTON, OPINION ON THE
CONSTITUTIONALITY OF THE BANK
OF THE UNITED STATES

Ideas have consequences," wrote the renowned conservative
scholar Richard M. Weaver in a book by that title.[1] Big ideas,
moreover, can have big consequences, and there are probably no
ideas in American political history bigger than the ones debated
by Alexander Hamilton and Thomas Jefferson at the time of the
founding. This battle of ideas—and it was indeed a battle—
formed the template for the debate over the role of government in
America that shapes our history to this day. The most important

idea of all, in the minds of Hamilton and Jefferson, was what kind of government Americans would live under.

Hamilton was one of the most influential figures in American political history. He served as a delegate at the Constitutional Convention of 1787; was one of the authors of *The Federalist Papers,* which helped convince the states to ratify the Constitution; and was the nation's first treasury secretary. Throughout these critical early years of the American republic, Hamilton made clear his political philosophy. To begin, he wanted a highly centralized government. He spoke out against the nation's first constitution, the Articles of Confederation, precisely because he felt it did not give enough power to the national government, and at the Constitutional Convention he proposed a *permanent* chief executive who could veto all state legislation—in other words, an American king. Hamilton wanted to use this centralized power to subsidize business in particular, and the more affluent in general, so as to make them supportive of an ever-growing state. As treasury secretary, he was a frenetic tax-increaser and advocated government planning of the economy. He championed the accumulation of public debt, protectionist tariffs, and politically controlled banks; belittled politicians like Jefferson who spoke too much of liberty; and believed that the new American government should pursue the course of national and imperial glory, just like the British, French, and Spanish empires.[2]

Thomas Jefferson held the exact opposite position on every one of these issues, and the two great men—who were also arch political rivals—clashed repeatedly. Jefferson championed limited, decentralized government, believing that history had shown that government had to be small and localized if individual liberty was to be protected. Thus he felt that most governmental functions should be the prerogative of the citizens of the sovereign states, not the central government. Unlike Hamilton, he was a "strict constructionist" with regard to the Constitution: he believed the national government had only those select powers (mostly for foreign affairs) that the sovereign states had expressly delegated to it in the Constitution; all others were reserved to the states respectively, or to the people, as enunciated in the Tenth Amendment.[3] Economically, he believed that laissez-faire was the surest route to peace and prosperity. As president, his top priority was to eliminate all internal taxes, many of which Hamilton had supported as President George Washington's treasury secretary. Jefferson was also a free trader and strongly opposed public debt and national banking as dire threats to natural rights. Finally, he believed that interfering in the affairs of other nations for the sake of "imperial glory" was a disastrous mistake.

Jefferson articulated his political philosophy in his first inaugural address, when he declared: "[A] wise and frugal Government, which shall restrain men from injuring one another, shall leave them otherwise free to regulate their own pursuits of industry and improvement, and shall not take from the mouth of labor the bread it has earned. This is the sum of good government." On another occasion he summed up his view even more succinctly: "That government is best which governs least." The motto of Hamilton, the consummate statist, might well have been "That government is best which governs *most*."

Of the two political rivals, it is Jefferson—the author of the Declaration of Independence and the third president of the United States—who is the better remembered today. But the reality is that Hamilton's vision, not Jefferson's, ultimately prevailed.

As the conservative columnist George F. Will has written, today "we honor Jefferson, but live in Hamilton's country."[4]

This is no cause for celebration. In fact, the triumph of Hamiltonianism has been mostly a curse on America.[5] The political legacy of Alexander Hamilton reads like a catalog of the ills of modern government: an out-of-control, unaccountable, monopolistic bureaucracy in Washington, D.C.; the demise of the Constitution as a restraint on the federal government's powers; the end of the idea that the citizens of the states should be the masters, rather than the servants, of their government; generations of activist federal judges who have eviscerated the constitutional protections of individual liberty in America; national debt; harmful protectionist international trade policies; corporate welfare (that is, the use of tax dollars to subsidize various politically connected businesses); and central economic planning and political control of the money supply, which have instigated boom-and-bust cycles in the economy.

The American Revolution was fought against a highly centralized state that was headed by a despotic chief executive who pulled the strings of the British mercantilist economic system (that is, a system built on protectionism, government franchise monopolies, a state-run bank, and interventionism that benefited the state and its supporters at the expense of the general public) as an instrument of plunder at the expense of the colonists. But Hamilton devoted the last quarter-century of his life to enshrining this very system in America. Thus Hamiltonianism— governmental consolidation, the elimination of true federalism, dominant executive power, and mercantilistic economic policies— amounted to nothing less than a betrayal of the principles for which Americans fought in the Revolution.

THE HAMILTON MYTHS

Alexander Hamilton's reputation has been propped up quite a bit in recent years, not least because he has been the subject of admiring biographies like Ron Chernow's 2004 blockbuster. But in the rush to reclaim the reputation of the man whom the neoconservative commentator David Brooks called "the most neglected" of the Founding Fathers, writers have clouded Hamilton's record and perpetuated a number of dangerous myths.[6]

For example, Chernow mislabeled Hamilton as "the prophet of the capitalist revolution in America," when in fact this founder's hyperinterventionist approach to the economy was anything *but* capitalism.[7] In reviewing Chernow's book and in at least one other column, Brooks, who proudly calls himself a "Hamiltonian," claimed that Hamilton somehow single-handedly "created capitalism."[8] The biographer Forrest McDonald made a similarly absurd assertion in giving Hamilton virtually all the credit for America's becoming "the richest, most powerful and freest nation in the history of the world."[9]

Another Hamilton biographer, the liberal political scientist Stephen F. Knott, recognized Hamilton as "the founder of a great republican empire," of "the America that explored the outer reaches of space, welcomed millions of immigrants, led the effort to defeat fascism and communism, produced countless technological advances, and abolished slavery and Jim Crow." *All* of this, Knott said, is "Hamilton's America."[10] This was very similar to the claim of the liberal author Michael Lind, who titled a book *Hamilton's Republic.* This collection of essays written by a variety of liberal thinkers celebrated Hamilton's influence on big-government heroes from Abraham Lincoln to Theodore Roosevelt and Franklin Roosevelt to Lyndon Johnson.

The liberal reverence for Hamilton's statism has progressed to the point that in 2006 the Brookings Institution, the nation's leading liberal think tank, initiated a new round of proposals for economic interventionism, social engineering, and bigger government, presumably to be the policy platform of the next Democratic administration. It was named "The Hamilton Project."[11]

As David Brooks's outspoken Hamiltonianism attests, praising Hamilton has become a bipartisan endeavor. Brooks and his fellow neoconservative William Kristol, editor of *The Weekly Standard* magazine, began their crusade for "national greatness conservatism" with a 1997 *Wall Street Journal* article that urged conservatives to reinvigorate "the nationalism of Alexander Hamilton and Henry Clay and Teddy Roosevelt."[12] Using the powers of the federal government to achieve some kind of "national greatness," as they favor, is vintage Hamiltonianism and could not possibly be farther from the Jeffersonian tradition, which held that government in a free society has no business engaging in such foibles.

It is no surprise that neoconservatives, who have never opposed big government in the way traditional conservatives have, would join the forces of Hamiltonian nationalists. But many other conservatives embrace Hamilton as well. For example, many so-called paleoconservatives, the most notable of whom is probably Patrick J. Buchanan, are Hamiltonians on economic policy because they support protectionism, tax subsidies for certain corporations, and economic interventionism generally. Even conservatives who supposedly champion the cause of limited constitutional government consider Hamilton one of their icons. In 1995, shortly after the Republican Party took over Congress promising to slash the size of the federal government, Speaker of the House Newt Gingrich told *Time* magazine that Hamilton was one of his personal heroes (followed by John Wayne, Kemal Atatürk, and Father Flanagan).[13]

Of course, the Gingrich Republicans never followed through on their anti–big government rhetoric; the federal government only became larger and more powerful after they took over Congress and the White House. Somehow, though, many American conservatives who believe, with Ronald Reagan, that government is usually the problem, not the solution, do not recognize that it was Hamilton more than anyone else who undid the restraints on the federal government that the framers of the Constitution so carefully put in place.

These conservatives would change their minds if they understood the *real* Hamilton.

HAMILTON'S LEGACY

This book is not a biography of Alexander Hamilton. Instead, it focuses on his core political and economic ideas; the intellectual, legal, and political battles over those ideas; and the consequences America has suffered since his ideas were implemented. The face-off between Hamilton and Jefferson, two brilliant and strong-willed men who grew to genuinely despise each other, is one of the most fascinating and consequential relationships in American history. But the debate did not die when Hamilton was killed in his famous duel with Aaron Burr in July 1804. In fact, it took the relentless efforts of generations of his political heirs to install Hamiltonianism for good in this country. As we will see, Hamiltonian hegemony would not be established in America until the second half of the nineteenth century, and the capstone on the

Hamiltonian revolution would not come until the early twentieth century.

The real Alexander Hamilton has receded from view, as historians and pundits cheerlead his "nationalism" and overlook most of what he actually said and did. Only by understanding the true significance of Hamilton can we ever hope to escape the clutches of Hamilton's curse and return to a constitutional republic more in line with the one the Founding Fathers designed—one that promoted and protected free enterprise and individual liberty.

CHAPTER 1

∿

The Rousseau of the Right

Hamilton, under the influence of the two political theorists most distasteful to Jefferson, Hobbes and Hume, was frankly the champion of the Leviathan State.

—JEFF TAYLOR, *WHERE DID THE PARTY GO?*
WILLIAM JENNINGS BRYAN, HUBERT HUMPHREY,
AND THE JEFFERSONIAN LEGACY

Alexander Hamilton was a brilliant man with boundless energy and ambition. Arguably no other founder has had a bigger impact on American society than he has. But that impact has been almost universally negative from the perspective of those who would like to think of America as the land of the free. Hamilton's main political and economic ideas were a combination of dictatorial monarchy, centralized power, imperialism, and economic mercantilism. These were the defining characteristics of the British Empire that the American revolutionaries had waged war against.

As a young man, Hamilton served heroically in the American Revolution and became a valuable aide to George Washington. Years after the war he continued to serve Washington, as America's first treasury secretary. And, of course, Hamilton was one of the principal authors of *The Federalist Papers*. In his private career he became a skilled lawyer and founder of the *New York Post* newspaper (founded for the purpose of smearing Jefferson) and the Bank of New York, institutions that still exist today. Although he was an unfaithful husband, his wife, who outlived him by more than fifty years, revered him, as did his children.

Hamilton was not a plantation owner like Jefferson, but an aristocratic New Yorker. Like Jefferson—and many other New York aristocrats—he was a slave owner who nevertheless at times spoke eloquently in opposition to the institution of slavery. This may sound surprising to most readers, but the fact is that slavery thrived for more than two hundred years in New York and was an integral part of the state's economy. As the Hamilton biographer Ron Chernow noted, "[S]lavery was well entrenched in much of the north" and "New York and New Jersey retained significant slave populations" long after the Revolution. "New York City, in particular, was identified with slavery . . . and was linked through its sugar refineries in the West Indies." (Hamilton was born and raised in Nevis, in the West Indies.) By the late 1790s one in five New York City households, like Hamilton's, "still held domestic slaves," who were "regarded as status symbols" by the wealthier and more aristocratic New Yorkers. Slavery was not ended in New York City until the early 1850s.[1]

Hamilton's wife, Eliza, was from a prominent and wealthy New York slave-owning family (the Schuylers) and retained some of the "house slaves" after marrying Hamilton. This fact is usually soft-pedaled by Hamilton's more worshipful biographers. "Hamilton . . . may have had a slave or two around the house" and "was too much a man of his age . . . to push for emancipation," wrote the Cornell University historian and Hamilton biographer Clinton Rossiter, a onetime editor of *The Federalist Papers.*[2] (Jefferson, on the other hand, endorsed a plan to end the slave trade early in the Revolution; condemned King George III for introducing slavery into America, in the first draft of the Declaration of Independence; laid out a plan for the abolition of slavery in Virginia, in *Notes on the State of Virginia;* and proposed blocking the spread of slavery in the Northwest Territory in 1784.)

Chernow oddly labels Hamilton an "abolitionist," despite the fact that he owned slaves and never endorsed abolition per se. He also bends over backward to downplay Hamilton's slave ownership, at one point arguing that, yes, he once purchased six slaves at a slave auction, but they were "probably" for his brother-in-law—as though that makes the purchase of human beings less immoral.[3]

Like virtually all politicians who rise to the highest levels of office, Alexander Hamilton was rather egomaniacal. "He never lacked of self-appreciation," William Graham Sumner wrote euphemistically in his 1905 biography.[4] Rossiter wrote of his "feverish, sometimes even grotesque concern for his reputation. Fame . . . was the spur of this remarkable man."[5] Other biographers have made similar observations.

So it is easy to understand why Thomas Jefferson thought of his political nemesis Hamilton as a deadly threat to American liberty: he was extremely intelligent and articulate; had an unmatched ego; spoke often of creating a government that would pursue "imperial glory" (and "glory" for himself as well); was a relentless statist, always and everywhere working to expand the size and scope of government (which to Jefferson meant less liberty for the individual); and worked tirelessly and effectively to achieve these ends. He was so effective, in fact, that Jefferson, in a letter to James Madison, once referred to him as a political "colossus."

Both men fully understood what was at stake: Would the American government mimic the British and pursue "national greatness," "imperial glory," and empire, as Hamilton preferred? Or would the primary purpose of government be the modest Jeffersonian one of protecting the lives, liberties, and property of its citizens? Both men understood that empire would mean that government would become the master, rather than servant, of the people, as it had been for generations in the Old World. It was the most important debate in American political history because its results would set the template, so to speak, of the young American government, the effects of which would be felt forever.

The founding generation certainly understood that the colonists of an empire could and would be treated as tax slaves or cannon fodder. This was the history of the Old World, and they had fought a revolution to escape such a fate. But the "national- ists," led by men like Hamilton and centered in New York and New England, also understood that life could be quite grand for those who managed and *ruled* over an empire. That was why his party—the Federalists—fought so hard and long for a much more powerful, consolidated, monopolistic government *and* for mercantilistic economic policies. New Englanders (and some New Yorkers) assumed that *they* were the salt of the earth, that *they* should rule America, and that glory and riches would be showered upon them if they captured the reins of government to pursue these ends. As the historian Clyde Wilson has noted, from the very beginning of the American republic New England "Yankees" (i.e., Federalists) regarded the new federal government . . . as an instrument to be used for their own purposes . . . In the first Congress, Yankees demanded that the federal government continue the British subsidies to their fishing fleets. While Virginia and the other Southern states gave up their vast western lands for future new states, New Englanders demanded a special preserve for themselves (the 'Western Reserve' in Ohio). . . . Under [President] John Adams, the New England quest for power grew into a frenzy. They passed the Sedition Law to punish anti-government words (as long as they controlled the government) in clear violation of the Constitution.[6]

HAMILTON THE NATIONALIST

Wilson has also made an important distinction between a "nationalist" and a patriot: "Patriotism is the wholesome, constructive love of one's land and people. Nationalism is the unhealthy love of one's government, accompanied by the aggressive desire to put down others—which becomes in deracinated modern men a substitute for religious faith. Patriotism is an appropriate, indeed necessary, sentiment for people who wish to preserve their freedom; nationalism is not."[7] Alexander Hamilton is generally acknowledged as being the most famous nationalist in American history.

To understand Hamilton's love of government, one merely has to read his own words. Hamilton disrespected Jefferson and his philosophy of freedom, complaining of "an excessive concern for liberty in public men."[8] Jefferson believed that government needed to be "bound by the chains of the Constitution," but

Hamilton viewed the Constitution quite the opposite way: as an instrument that could "legitimize" virtually any act of government if given the "proper" interpretation by clever lawyers like himself and his fellow Federalists. When Jefferson's view prevailed, especially after his election as president in 1800, Hamilton denounced the Constitution as "a frail and worthless fabric." To Hamilton, it was "worthless" as long as it was used to restrain rather than expand the state.

As Clinton Rossiter explained, "Hamilton's overriding purpose was to build the foundations of a new empire."[9] He dreamed of governmental "glory" that "could reach out forcefully and benevolently to every person," said Rossiter.[10] (Never mind that force and benevolence are more often than not opposites.)

Far from accepting Jefferson's limited-government philosophy, Hamilton incessantly complained of the lack of "energy" in government. As Rossiter observed, Hamilton had an "obsession with the idea of political energy," feared "weakness in government," and condemned constitutional constraints on governmental power as "a pernicious dream." Hamilton, Rossiter said, "had perhaps the highest respect for government of any important American political thinker *who ever lived*" (emphasis added).[11]

"We must have a government of more power," Hamilton wrote to George Washington in August 1780. This statement marked the beginning of his lengthy campaign against America's first constitution, the Articles of Confederation.[12] To Hamilton's and other Federalists' claims that the government needed to be more powerful and consolidated, Patrick Henry sagely responded that the government under the Articles of Confederation was powerful enough to have created and supplied an army that defeated the British Empire. Nevertheless Hamilton's agitating paid off, as seven years later he got the Constitutional Convention he had long been proposing. Supposedly the convention was intended to amend the Articles of Confederation, but, of course, the Articles would end up being scrapped completely. What Hamilton and his political compatriots wanted was a much more highly centralized government with vastly expanded executive branch powers.

Discarding the Articles of Confederation was not the work of the Jeffersonians. "States' rights" meant to Jefferson and his followers that the only way to have citizens control their own government would be through political communities organized at the state and local levels of government. Thus Jeffersonians insisted that as many governmental functions as possible be conducted by the governmental units that are closest to the people—namely, the states and localities. That was why, after the Constitution was ratified, Jefferson believed the Tenth Amendment, which reserved all powers not specifically delegated to the central government to the people and the states, was the most important part of the entire document. He understood that throughout the history of Western civilization, freedom came only through the dispersal of political power, not through its consolidation in a few hands.

In explaining the significance of the Tenth Amendment in a private correspondence, Jefferson wrote in 1824 that "[w]ith respect to our State and federal governments, I do not think their relations correctly understood by foreigners. They generally suppose the former is subordinate to the latter. But this is not the case. They are coordinate departments of one . . . integral whole. To the

State governments are reserved all legislation and administration, in affairs which concern their own citizens only, and to the federal government is given whatever concerns foreigners, or the citizens of other States."[13]

The Constitutional Convention of 1787 was held in secret, and there was apparently an agreement that what went on there would not be made public until after the death of all the participants. But by the 1820s word finally began to seep out. First the notes of one of the convention's delegates, Robert Yates (who would serve as chief justice of New York from 1790 to 1798), were published under the title *Secret Proceedings and Debates of the Constitutional Convention*. Yates died in 1801, and his notes became the property of his widow, who eventually allowed their publication. They were edited by one John Lansing, who was chancellor of the state of New York and had also attended the Constitutional Convention. Then in 1823 Senator John Taylor of Virginia authored *New Views of the Constitution of the United States*, which relied heavily on Yates's notes.[14]

What these books revealed was how quickly Hamilton moved to consolidate political power in the hands of the central government—and, more specifically, in the hands of the executive branch. At the convention Hamilton proposed a *permanent* president and senate, with all political power in the national government, as far away as possible from the people, and centered in the executive. He also wanted "all laws of the particular states, contrary to the constitution or laws of the United States [government], to be utterly void," and he proposed that "the governor . . . of each state shall be appointed by the general government, and shall have a negative [i.e, a veto] upon the laws about to be passed in the state of which he is governor."[15]

Such proposals prompted Clinton Rossiter to write, in an extraordinary display of euphemism, "Hamilton looked to the executive branch as the chief source of political energy."[16] In plainer language, Hamilton proposed a kind of "king" who would yield supreme power over all the people, who in turn would have essentially no say in how their government was run. The states would be mere provinces whose governors would be appointed by and loyal to the "king." Under such a regime, *all* political power in the nation would be exercised by the chief executive and his circle of advisers, which would undoubtedly have included Alexander Hamilton as perhaps the chief adviser. John Taylor correctly noted that what was being proposed was "a national government, nearly conforming to that of England. . . . By Colonel Hamilton's project, the states were fairly and openly to be restored to the rank of provinces and to be made as dependent upon a supreme national government, as they had been upon a supreme British government."[17]

But the convention did not embrace Hamilton's plan for executive dictatorship and monopoly government. Quoting Yates's journal, Taylor noted that the convention attendees viewed the Constitution as a compact among the free and independent states and not as the creation of a "national" government. "[I]t was proposed and seconded," Taylor wrote, "to erase the word *national*, and substitute the words United States [in the plural] in the fourth resolution, which passed in the affirmative. Thus, we see an opinion expressed at the convention, that the phrase 'United States' did not mean a consolidated American people or nation, and all the inferences in favour of a national government . . . are overthrown."[18]

The language of "United States" in the plural is most significant: as revealed by Taylor and others, it meant that the convention delegates (and most everyone else) understood that the free, independent, and sovereign states were united in a confederacy that would delegate a few selected powers to the central government, primarily for national defense and foreign affairs. (This was what the Constitution's Supremacy Clause documented.) They did *not* create a consolidated government called "the United States." Nor did they create a central government whose laws would always trump the laws of the states. (The Supremacy Clause allows for national "supremacy" only for the specific powers that are expressly delegated to the federal government. All others are reserved to the states and the people under the Tenth Amendment. Taylor himself documented that this was the understanding at the Constitutional Convention.)[19]

As Taylor, Yates, and other Jeffersonians observed, Hamilton and his party combined economic interventionism with their quest for consolidated or monopolistic governmental power. They did not want to allow the independent states to dissent from their high-tariff policies, for example. Protectionist tariffs to allow (mostly northern state) manufacturers to monopolize their industries, isolated from European competition, could not work if some of the states chose a low-tariff policy. Imports would flood into the low-tariff states, and then become dispersed throughout the nation by merchants. This was why a monopolistic, consolidated government, with all power in the nation's capital, was their main goal.

To Taylor and the Jeffersonians, this scheme was essentially "Monarchy, and its hand-maiden consolidation, and its other hand-maiden, ambition, and a national government" dressed up in "popular disguises" such as "national splendor" and "national strength."[20] The "pretended national prosperity," Taylor added, "was only a pretext of ambition and monopoly . . . intended to feed avarice, gratify ambition, and make one portion of the nation tributary to another."[21] Thus, as early as 1823 southerners like Senator John Taylor suspected that northern politicians were conspiring to use the powers of the central government to tax one portion of the country—the South—for the benefit of their own region. (This was long before there were any significant northern abolitionist movements.)

Taylor noted that the proponents of consolidation relied on "paradoxical" arguments. They contended, he said, "that the greater the [government] revenue, the richer are the people; that frugality in the government is an evil; in the people, a good; . . . that monopolies and exclusive privileges are general welfare; that a division of sovereignty will raise up a class of wicked, intriguing, self-interested politicians in the states; and that human nature will be cleansed of these propensities by a sovereignty consolidated in one government."[22]

Of course, Hamilton's scheme for the Constitutional Convention failed. Taylor observed that "Colonel Hamilton . . . seems to have quitted the convention in despair" soon after "the failure of the project."[23] But Hamilton and his followers did realize some "progress" at the convention, as the citizens of the sovereign states delegated more powers to the central government (for their own benefit, with the government acting *as their agent*) than the Articles of Confederation did.

What's more, the nationalists did not give up the fight once the Constitution was completed. Hamilton, as is well known, campaigned aggressively for ratification of the Constitution as one of the lead authors of *The Federalist Papers*. Many of these writings sounded quite Jeffersonian, but his actions during the actual convention, as they would be exposed decades later, suggest that such positioning was less than sincere. More likely, his writings were intended to goad the public into acquiescing in the adoption of a document that he hoped would become a "living constitution." In his preface to *The Federalist,* the historian Richard B. Morris wrote that Hamilton "constantly sought to reassure the states' rights politicians [the Jeffersonians] that state sovereignty would not be jeopardized" by the new Constitution; yet he hoped to *abolish* state sovereignty once the Constitution was adopted.[24] He also promised, during the constitutional debates at the New York ratifying convention, that the U.S. Congress would never contemplate "marching the troops of one state into the bosom of another" for any reason.[25] But as we will see, when he became treasury secretary he personally accompanied President George Washington and some thirteen thousand (mostly conscripted) troops into Pennsylvania to attempt to quell the so-called Whiskey Rebellion.

Hamilton had laid out his most desired political framework at the Constitutional Convention. His followers and political heirs would work relentlessly for decades in the trenches of the Federalist, Whig, and eventually Republican parties to finally achieve their goal of a monopolistic central state that would enact interventionist economic policies.

"FOR THE PUBLIC GOOD"

Hundreds of years of history—and the rule over the colonists by the British government—had taught Jefferson that the closer government is to the people, the more likely it is to be the servant rather than the master of the people. The converse is also true:

despotism is the inevitable consequence of consolidated governmental power. The British historian Lord Acton's famous declaration about how power corrupts would, in the late nineteenth century, enunciate what Jefferson knew in his bones: "[W]here you have a concentration of power in a few hands, all too frequently men with the mentality of gangsters get control. History has proven that. All power tends to corrupt; absolute power corrupts absolutely."

The founding generation understood this as well as anyone. (And, of course, Lord Acton's dictum was proven true over and over again during the twentieth century. The worst tyrants of that era were consolidationists and enemies of federalism or states' rights.) Thus nationalists like Alexander Hamilton faced a major problem in trying to convince the public to trust centralized government power. To overcome this problem, they relied on a rhetorical gimmick, endlessly repeating that if all political power were consolidated in their hands and the government given more "energy," then they could be trusted to serve "the general will" and not their own self-interests. They disagreed, in other words, with James Madison's dictum in *The Federalist Papers* that if men were angels, there would be no need for government at all. They promised to behave in an angelic manner "for the public good" if they were given enough power.

This Hamiltonian propaganda tactic was almost identical to the methods of the French Jacobins. While Hamilton and his fellow Federalists ironically smeared Jefferson with the label "Jacobin," because of Jefferson's friendships with the French, in fact it was Hamilton who espoused the Jacobin philosophy, as first expressed by the eighteenth-century French philosopher Jean-Jacques Rousseau.

Rousseau's main idea was the supposed existence of a "general will." That will is not necessarily expressed by the general public in any way but is presumed to be known by the ruling elite. With Rousseau, "no aspect of human life is excluded from the control of the general will," and "whosoever refuses to obey the general will must in that instance be restrained by the body politic, which actually means that he is forced to be free."[26]

Jefferson, Madison, and other founders denied the existence of any such will. Indeed, as the political philosopher Claes Ryn has pointed out, this view of government "collides head on with advocates of constitutionalism," such as the majority of the American founders.[27] "Rousseau's wish to . . . dissolve the people into a homogeneous mass, abolish decentralization, and remove representative institutions could not be in sharper contrast to American traditions of constitutionalism, federalism, localism, and representation."[28]

The Jeffersonians "hated and feared" the Jacobin concept of a "general will," wrote Felix Morley in *Freedom and Federalism*.[29] For if "the general will" were to become a practical reality regarding the operation of government, then all voluntary associations must be subjected to government regulation and control in the name of "the people" and their "will"—as interpreted by a ruling elite. This would be the road to serfdom and the end of individual liberty.

In *Alexander Hamilton and the Constitution*, Clinton Rossiter wrote that "throughout his life, [Hamilton] . . . stated his belief in the existence of 'the public interest.'" It was "the streak of political Romanticism that ran all through this area of thought."[30] This is undoubtedly why the political scientist Cecelia Kenyon labeled

Hamilton "the Rousseau of the Right" in the scholarly journal *Political Science Quarterly.*[31]

Rossiter cataloged how some version of "the general will" appears hundreds of times in Hamilton's speeches, letters, and writings. Among the phrases he used were "the public good," "the public interest," "the public weal," "the public safety," "the public welfare," "the public felicity," "the public happiness," "the general good," "the general interest," "the common interest," "the national interest," "the national happiness," "the welfare of the community," "the true interests of the community," "the permanent welfare of society," "the good of the whole community," and "the common interests of humanity." The last phrase, said Rossiter, was "a burst of supra-nationalism."[32] Hamilton, "more pointedly than any other political thinker of his time, introduced the concept of the 'public good' into American thought."[33]

To claim that government policies that benefit small but powerful special interests at the expense of the rest of society are really "in the public interest" is an ancient political tactic. It was employed, for example, by the British mercantilists of Hamilton's time (and before) to argue that high food prices caused by protectionist trade policies were somehow in the general public's best interest. But no government policy can be said to be in "the public interest" unless it benefits every member of the public. And this is a rare if not nonexistent occurrence in any democracy. All democracies evolve into a state where the net beneficiaries of government (those who receive more in benefits than they pay in taxes) outnumber and dominate the net taxpayers (those who pay more in taxes than they receive in benefits).

As will be discussed extensively in this book, Hamilton was

an American mercantilist, and he and his party (and its political heirs, the Whigs and Republicans) advocated special-interest policies that would primarily benefit politically connected merchants, manufacturers, speculators, and bankers at the expense of the rest of the public. The "public interest" rhetoric was (and is) an indispensable political smoke screen if they were to achieve political success. The wool must be pulled over the public's eyes with "public interest" rhetoric if mercantilism were to succeed. Jefferson and his political compatriots, such as John Taylor, saw through it. Taylor, in fact, wrote an entire book attacking the Federalists' mercantilistic economic views, entitled *Tyranny Unmasked*.[34]

THE FOUNDING FATHER OF CONSTITUTIONAL SUBVERSION

Having failed to create a "national" government at the Constitutional Convention, Alexander Hamilton denounced the document as "a frail and worthless fabric" and devoted himself to "reinterpreting" the "real meaning" of the document so as to subvert it. His purpose was essentially to rewrite the Constitution through lawyerly manipulation of its words to satisfy his main purpose of building "the foundations of a new empire," as Clinton Rossiter called it.

Hamilton's expansive view of the Constitution stood in stark contrast to Jefferson's strict constructionism. Jefferson believed— and the Constitutional Convention had affirmed—that the citizens of the free, independent, and sovereign states had delegated a few powers to the central government *for their own mutual benefit*, but that citizens of the states, rather than the central government, remained sovereign. He recognized the Constitution as necessary for constraining government and even supported secession in instances when the government no longer behaved in a constitutional manner (not at all a surprising position for the author of the American Declaration of Secession from the British Empire).

But Hamilton dismissed Jefferson's strict constructionism and viewed the Constitution as a grant of powers rather than as a set of limitations. With clever manipulation of words, he believed, the Constitution could be used to approve virtually all government actions without involving the citizens at all. "It seems certain," Rossiter wrote, "that Hamilton would have affixed a certain certificate of constitutionality to every last tax. . . . Hamilton took a large view of the power of Congress to tax because he took a large view of the power to spend."[35]

The Constitution had an amendment process, of course, but amending the Constitution would have required Hamilton to sell his Leviathan State ideas to the American public. Rossiter rightly observed: "Having failed to persuade his colleagues at Philadelphia of the beauties of a truly national plan of government, and having thereafter recognized the futility of persuading the legislatures of three-fourths of the states to surrender even a jot of their privileges, he set out to remold the Constitution into an instrument of national supremacy."[36] The Federalist Party's "lawyereaucracy" would have to "amend" the Constitution in a more clandestine way.

Many of Hamilton's arguments are repeated to this day by academics, politicians, and others who favor a bigger, more activist government with unbridled executive powers. For example, Hamilton set out to rewrite the history of the American founding by arguing that the citizens of the states had never been sovereign. On June 29, 1787, he said that the states were merely "artificial beings" that had nothing to do with creating the union.[37] In a speech before the New York State Assembly in that same year he argued that the "nation," and not the states, had "full power of sovereignty" dating back even before the Articles of Confederation; he actually called that first constitution an "abridgement" of "the original sovereignty of the Union."[38] (Abraham Lincoln would make the exact same argument in his first inaugural address seventy-four years later. It was the basis for his denial of state sovereignty—and the right of secession—and his military invasion of the southern states.)

This is perhaps the biggest lie in American political history. But the myth would be endlessly repeated by Hamilton's political heirs, the Whigs and Republicans, up through the Lincoln regime and beyond, to this very day.

Hamilton also invented the myth that the Constitution somehow grants the federal government "implied powers." "Implied powers" are powers that are not actually in the Constitution but that statists like Hamilton *wish* were there. As Rossiter pointed out, "One finds elaborations of this doctrine throughout his writings as Secretary of the Treasury."[39] The most notable articulation of this idea can be found in Hamilton's *Opinion on the Constitutionality of the Bank of the United States*. He wrote this report in 1791, while serving as treasury secretary. President Washington had asked both Hamilton and Jefferson for their opinions on the subject. In his opinion, Hamilton wrote that "there are *implied*, as well as *express powers* [in the Constitution], and that the *former* are as effectually delegated as the latter" (emphasis in original).[40] He added, "Implied powers are to be considered as delegated [to the federal government] equally with express ones." A nationalized bank, he went on to argue, was one of these implied powers.

Jefferson vehemently disagreed, arguing that the express powers delegated to the federal government in Article I, Section 8, of the Constitution (providing for the national defense, coining of money, etc.) were expressly stated because they were the *only* powers delegated to the federal government by the sovereign states that ratified the Constitution. Any new powers, Jefferson believed, could be delegated only by a constitutional amendment. He realized that such a doctrine as "implied powers" would essentially render the Constitution useless as a tool for limiting government if the limits of government were simply left up to the imaginations of ambitious politicians like Hamilton.

Hamilton prevailed, however, and "with the aid of the doctrine of implied powers," wrote Clinton Rossiter, he "converted the . . . powers enumerated in Article I, Section 8 into firm foundations for whatever prodigious feats of legislation any future Congress might contemplate."[41] Jefferson's worst fear was realized. As we will discuss in detail in Chapter 4, the shock troops of the Federalist Party—federally appointed judges—would use Hamilton's arguments to essentially rewrite history and the Constitution. Thus was "liberal judicial activism" born.

Another Federalist, President John Adams, tried to achieve just this goal when he appointed hundreds of "midnight judges" to the federal judiciary during the very last hours of his administration. With Jefferson about to be inaugurated as president, the Federalists hoped that all those politically loyal judges would subvert the new administration's strict construction of the Constitution and its limited government policies. When Jefferson opposed them and succeeded in getting rid of most of the judges, his political enemies argued that he was waging a "war on the judiciary." To this day, nationalist historians repeat this myth. Of course, Jefferson was waging war not on the judiciary as a whole but only on politically appointed judges who were determined to subvert the U.S. Constitution in the service of big government.

George Washington had condemned the notion of a "living constitution" in his Farewell Address (which, oddly enough, is said to have been at least partly ghostwritten by Hamilton). In that address President Washington said, "If in the opinion of the People, the distribution of modification of the Constitutional powers be in any particular wrong, let it be corrected by an amendment in the way the Constitution designates. But let there be no change by usurpation . . . the customary weapon by which free governments are destroyed."[42] Hamilton's theory of implied powers ignored this warning, laying the template for generations of lawyers who would use the courts, rather than the formal amendment process, to essentially render the constitutional constraints on government null and void.

Not only were there supposedly "implied" powers in the Constitution that only the wise and lawyerly like Hamilton recognized (but that were foreign to James Madison, who like Jefferson was a strict constructionist), there were also "resulting powers," Hamilton argued. If the United States ever conquered one of their neighboring countries, he wrote, "they would possess sovereign jurisdiction over the conquered territory. This would be rather the result from the whole mass of the government . . . than a consequence of . . . powers specially enumerated."[43]

Thus, if the government engaged in an unconstitutional

war of conquest and succeeded, the unconstitutional "powers" would magically become constitutional, in Hamilton's opinion. Taken to its logical ends, this argument implies that *any* action of government would be de facto "constitutional" by virtue of the fact that the action occurred. This is how Hamilton viewed the Constitution—as a potential blank check for unlimited powers of government.

Jefferson and Madison were such strict constructionists, by contrast, that each of them, as president, opposed the expenditure of tax dollars even on relatively modest road- and canal-building projects by saying that the Constitution did not expressly name such things as legitimate governmental functions. The Constitution would have to first be amended, they argued.

The Federalists at the Constitutional Convention had known what they were doing when they inserted the General Welfare Clause into the Constitution. ("The Congress shall have Power To lay and collect Taxes, Duties, Imposts and Excises, to pay the Debts and provide for the common Defence and general Welfare of the United States.") Hamilton would immediately use it to expand the powers of the central government. The main source of Hamilton's expansive interpretation of the General Welfare Clause is his famous *Report on Manufactures,* which he delivered to Congress in late 1791 while serving as secretary of the treasury.

In that report Hamilton advocated having the federal government grant "pecuniary bounties" to the manufacturers of certain items (a practice known today as "corporate welfare"). Jefferson and Madison objected that nothing in the Constitution permitted such an expenditure of tax dollars. Hamilton's report cited the General Welfare Clause to handle such objections: "[T]he power to *raise money* is *plenary and indefinite* [in the Constitution]," he wrote. "The terms *general Welfare* were doubtless intended to signify more than was expressed." He claimed, "It is therefore of necessity left to the discretion of the National Legislature, to pronounce upon the objects, which concern the general Welfare, and for which . . . an appropriation of money is requisite and proper." Otherwise, he wrote, "numerous exigencies incident to the affairs of a nation would have been left without a provision."[44]

"Thus with a flourish," wrote Rossiter, "did Hamilton convert the fuzzy words about the 'general Welfare' from a 'sort of caption,' as Madison described them, into a grant of almost unlimited authority [to the federal government] to enact programs that would divert the growing riches of the American people [through taxation]."[45] In Hamilton's rendering, the federal government's powers were virtually unlimited; after all, the case will always be made by *some* politicians that virtually everything government does advances the "general welfare" of the country. Before long, the "National Legislature" was frequently using the General Welfare Clause to justify programs that served *special interests* rather than the "general welfare." By the middle of the nineteenth century the problem had become so evident that when the Confederate government adopted its own constitution in 1861, the document was almost a carbon copy of the U.S. Constitution—*minus the General Welfare Clause.* What is more, generations of nationalist judges have used Hamilton's argument to expand the size and scope of government far beyond what the Constitution allows.

Hamilton was also likely the first to twist the meaning of the

Commerce Clause of the Constitution. ("The Congress shall have Power . . . To regulate Commerce with foreign Nations, and among the several States.") This clause was supposed to give the central government the ability to regulate interstate commerce to promote free trade between the states. But Hamilton asserted that "commerce" was really an all-inclusive term for *all* commercial activities in society, and therefore that the government had a "right" to regulate and control *all* commerce, not just interstate trade but *intra*state commerce as well.[46]

Jefferson had argued that there was no constitutional authority to regulate commerce *within* states, as a nationalized bank would do. Hamilton, in his *Opinion on the Constitutionality of the Bank of the United States,* responded by saying that the Commerce Clause authorized a national bank. Since Congress was authorized to regulate commerce "upon the whole," he claimed, it was therefore also authorized to regulate "every part" of "the whole." In other words, he insisted that *any* regulation of commerce, even interstate commerce, would somehow affect intrastate commerce, and so the Commerce Clause in reality empowered Congress to control the latter too. Hamilton's language is rather convoluted by modern standards, but here's how he made his case: "What regulation of commerce does not extend to the internal commerce of every State? What are all the duties upon imported articles, amounting to prohibitions, but so many bounties upon domestic manufactures, affecting the interests of different classes of citizens, in different ways? . . . In short, what regulation of trade between the States but must affect the internal trade of each State? What can operate upon the whole but must extend to every part?"[47]

In Hamilton's opinion, then, the Commerce Clause allowed

for government planning of every economic enterprise. No wonder Jefferson, Madison, and other devotees of the Constitution thought of Hamilton as a deadly enemy of the free society. For example, in a September 9, 1792, letter to President Washington, Jefferson wrote that "I have utterly . . . disapproved of the system of the Secretary of Treasury. . . . His system [of a national bank, corporate welfare, public debt, protectionist tariffs, etc.] flowed from principles averse to liberty, & was calculated to undermine and demolish the republic, by creating an influence of his department over the members of the legislature."[48]

It was also Hamilton who invented the theory of "war powers." The Constitution does give the central government the power to "provide for the common Defence," but Hamilton interpreted that to mean that *unlimited* resources should be given to the military, including conscription and a standing army in peacetime. (The Constitution itself specifically limited the existence of a standing army to two years.) In *Federalist* no. 23 Hamilton wrote that the resources of the military "ought to exist without limitation." He also wanted government to nationalize all industries related to the military, which in today's world would mean virtually all industries.

Jefferson and his followers opposed this fanciful interpretation of the Constitution as well. Drawing on the lessons of history, they understood that standing armies are a potentially bankrupting drain on the nation and also that governments throughout history had used such armies against their own people for such purposes as tax collection or just plain intimidation. Their own experience was particularly instructive: the American colonists were the victims of such intimidation at the hands of the British army. That's one reason why the Constitution allowed for only a two-year standing army.

Jefferson articulated his opposition to a standing army in his first annual message to Congress as president, on December 8, 1801. President Jefferson declared that it is neither "needful or safe that a standing army should be kept up in time of peace" and that "the only force which can be ready at every point," should an enemy choose to invade, "is the body of neighboring citizens formed into a militia."[49] Then, in an April 12, 1802, letter to General Thaddeus Kosciusko of Poland, who had inquired about whether some Polish military officers could "expect to be employed" in America, Jefferson wrote: "I hasten to inform you, that we are now actually engaged in reducing our military establishment one third . . . We keep in service no more than men enough to garrison the small posts dispersed at great distances on our frontiers."[50]

WHY HAMILTON LED AN INVASION OF HIS OWN COUNTRY

Many of Hamilton's key political supporters—and friends, business associates, and relatives—were holders of federal bonds (especially war bonds). More government revenue was needed, Hamilton believed, so that these government bondholders could be paid their principal and interest. In addition, Hamilton believed in issuing even more bonds for the sake of enlarging the public debt. He thought this would tie the wealthy of the country (who would be the primary purchasers of government bonds) to the government, thereby creating a formidable political pressure group in favor of bigger government and higher taxation.

So as U.S. treasury secretary in the Washington administration, Hamilton was instrumental in getting Congress to enact numerous excise taxes, a national property tax, and other taxes, including a special tax on whiskey.

In western Pennsylvania farmers used whiskey as a form of "currency" or barter with which they bought needed goods, since the wheat and other grains they grew were too cumbersome and expensive to transport in order to engage in trade. The Pennsylvania farmers naturally believed that the whiskey tax was grossly inequitable, for farmers in, say, South Carolina and Virginia were not paying a special tax on cotton and tobacco. They refused to pay the tax, generally revolting against it, and even tarred and feathered federal tax collectors whenever they showed up.

Some statesmen, such as Secretary of State Edmund Randolph (formerly the attorney general), urged negotiations between the federal government and the Pennsylvanians. But Hamilton, writes William Hogeland in *The Whiskey Rebellion*, was "arguing for moving immediately, with an overwhelming force of at least twelve thousand men, bigger than any American army to date, more than had beaten the British at Yorktown."[51] So at Hamilton's urging, President Washington personally led an army of more than 13,000 *conscripts* to Pennsylvania, accompanied by Hamilton the chief tax collector. Hamilton's main purpose, writes Hogeland, was apparently "to frighten the states with the threat of a military takeover" by a federal army if they resisted taxation, however unjust it seemed to them.[52] This fact speaks volumes about why Hamilton was such a vociferous proponent of a standing army. He wanted a standing army of *tax collectors*. This is how King George III collected stamp taxes and other levies from the

American colonists prior to the Revolution, and it is how Hamilton intended to collect his whiskey tax.

James Madison remarked that Hamilton's extreme "excitement" over this whole affair exposed his not-so-hidden agenda of "the glories of a United States woven together by a system of tax collectors."[53] (It was also Madison who had argued in favor of the Second Amendment's right to bear arms for the purpose of fending off such an invasion of a sovereign state by the central government.) In his history of the Federalist Party, the historian John C. Miller noted that Jefferson's party had "suspicions that the army had been strengthened in 1798 not to fight Frenchmen but to suppress opposition to Federalist policies."[54] He matter-of-factly concluded that "when the French failed to invade the United States and Hamilton's dream of foreign adventures went glimmering, the most compelling reason for maintaining a large military establishment was to back up Federal tax collectors, district attorneys, and judges, in the enforcement of unpopular laws."[55] All in "the public interest," in Hamilton's view.

The rank-and-file soldiers may have been mostly conscripts, but many of the *officers* who accompanied Hamilton and Washington to Pennsylvania were "from the ranks of the creditor aristocracy in the seaboard cities," as Claude Bowers wrote in *Jefferson and Hamilton*. These officers were eager to enforce collection of the whiskey tax so that the value of their government bond holdings could be enhanced and secured.[56] They were, in Bowers's words, "of the first Philadelphia families in wealth, gorgeous in their blue uniforms made of the finest broadcloth, all mounted on magnificent bay horses so nearly uniform in size and color that any two of them would make a fine span of coach horses. A proud show they made with their superb trappings, their silver-mounted stirrups and martingales, their drawn swords glistening in the sun," like "patrician conquerors."[57]

These "conquerors" treated their captives—including "old men who had fought for American independence . . . some pale and sick"—most inhumanely. The tax protesters were "run through the snow in chains, toward various lockups in town jails, stables, and cattle pens, to await interrogation by Hamilton."[58] This went on all the way across the state of Pennsylvania, until they reached Philadelphia.

Washington apparently lost interest in the affair and returned home, leaving Hamilton in charge. He played the role of Grand Inquisitor and "prompted detainees to manufacture evidence" against his political opponents from Pennsylvania. One of his assistants, a General White, "ordered the beheading of anyone attempting to escape" and was not overruled by the treasury secretary, who was apparently willing to play judge, jury, and executioner, if need be.[59] Indeed, Hamilton *ordered* local judges to render guilty verdicts against the twenty men who were eventually imprisoned, and he wanted all guilty parties to be *hanged.* But only twelve individuals went to trial; two men were convicted, and George Washington pardoned them both, to the extreme disappointment of his young treasury secretary.

So the whiskey rebels prevailed. They did *not* pay the whiskey tax; *no one* was successfully prosecuted; and once Jefferson became president, the hated whiskey tax, along with most other excise taxes, was abolished.

Hamilton never stopped his quest for "national" and "imperial" glory, though. After his march on Pennsylvania he called for war with France. Apparently exasperated with his political enemies from Virginia, especially Jefferson and Madison, he also spoke of leading a federal army into Virginia to put the state "to the test."[60] This test would eventually occur when another Hamiltonian nationalist, Abraham Lincoln, carried it out in 1861.

CHAPTER 2

∼

Public Blessing or National Curse?

A national debt, if it is not excessive, will be to us a public blessing.
—ALEXANDER HAMILTON

I consider the fortunes of our republic as depending, in an eminent degree, on the extinguishment of the public debt.
—THOMAS JEFFERSON

Government debt is every politician's dream: it gives him the ability to buy votes by spending on government programs (with funds raised through borrowing) that will make him popular now, while putting the lion's share of the cost on future taxpayers, who must pay off the debt through taxes. It is the ultimate political something-for-nothing scheme. Furthermore, the costs of servicing the debt are so widely dispersed among the taxpayers that hardly anyone realizes that his taxes are higher because of the debt service. Government bondholders are typically paid out of general revenues, and there is no way of knowing how much of your taxes are for debt service rather than national defense, the judicial system, and so forth. American taxpayers have never been presented with itemized federal tax bills.

This creates what contemporary economists call a "fiscal illusion"—namely, it makes government *appear* to be less costly than it really is. Consequently, the taxpayers are duped into acquiescing in bigger government than they would if they had a clearer picture of the true costs of government. And the chickens eventually come home to roost: at this writing American politicians have accumulated so much debt that every baby born in America has as his or her share of it a six-figure sum, payable over his or her lifetime in taxes.

In his 1997 book on the history of the national debt, John Steele Gordon calculated that, as of that moment, the $5.1 trillion debt "laid out in silver dollars . . . would be about 120 million miles long, wrapping around the equator 5,000 times."[1] As of 2007 the national debt exceeded $9 trillion. And if one counts the unfunded liabilities (i.e., promises to pay) of just the government's Medicare, pension, and Social Security programs, the government debt is in the range of $70 trillion.

Taxpayers can occasionally be tricked into supporting even the biggest government program of all—war—if the direct costs to them can be hidden well enough through borrowing. There would not be as many wars, and the ones that do occur would likely be shorter, if they were paid for through direct taxation. Taxpayers feeling the sting of gigantic wartime tax increases would be much more inclined to pressure their governmental representatives to limit their military adventures to national defense purposes, as opposed to imperialistic ventures based on more dubious motives. Americans may agree with the goal of "spreading democracy around the globe" as long as they believe that it won't cost them much (or anything). Present them with an explicit tax bill for it, however, and many of them will reverse their opinion.

All of this was understood in Hamilton's time, which is why so many of his contemporaries opposed the accumulation of government debt. In response to an inquiry about the use of debt to finance the War of 1812, Jefferson wrote on June 24, 1813, that "the perpetuation of debt, has drenched the earth with blood."[2] He was referring to the fact that use of government debt to finance wars had made it all too easy for European monarchs to engage in perpetual wars of conquest. He believed that if government was to borrow money during an emergency, such as a war, it should simultaneously tax *current* taxpayers to pay off the debt and not impose the burden on future generations: "It is a wise rule . . . never to borrow a dollar without laying a tax in the same instant or paying the interest annually, and the principal within a given term."[3] In such instances he favored limiting the government debt to nineteen years so as not to burden the next generation. As president he oversaw a significant reduction of the national debt.

Hamilton, meanwhile, *championed* the creation of a large national debt. He viewed it as an indispensable instrument for growing the state in general, not just as a mechanism for paying off war debts. It would give the government infinitely more "energy." Of course, Hamilton qualified his praise for a national debt by saying "if it is not excessive." But could a man of his intelligence and understanding of government, one of the authors of *The Federalist Papers,* seriously believe that government debt, once established, would not inevitably become "excessive"? Indeed, he devoted most of his adult life to promoting excessive government. It is a red herring argument to say that Hamilton was in favor of only "nonexcessive" government debt. Once the floodgates of government borrowing were opened, there would be no shutting them. History has borne this out, and had borne it out for centuries as of Hamilton's time.

HAMILTON'S FIRST FINANCIAL CAPER

Upon becoming the nation's first treasury secretary, Hamilton "speedily made [the Treasury Department] the most important office in the government," in the words of William Graham Sumner.[4] He frenetically wrote several major "reports" to Congress urging it to adopt a policy of debt, higher taxation, central banking, protectionism, and tax-funded subsidies for businesses (i.e., "corporate welfare").[5]

Hamilton wrote two separate reports advocating government debt. The first called for the new government to assume all the old government debt, something that hardly anyone disagreed with. New bonds would be issued, backed by revenue from the new tariff that Hamilton was instrumental in putting into place. The old war debt was to be cashed out at full face value. This plan "immediately became public knowledge in New York City," wrote John Steele Gordon, "but news of it spread only slowly, via horseback and sailing vessel, to the rest of the country."[6] This in turn created tremendous speculative opportunities for Hamilton's New York City and New England friends and supporters, including the financier Robert Morris (who was Hamilton's legislative liaison in the U.S. Senate) and Hamilton's father-in-law, Philip Schuyler, among many others.

New York speculators, having been given this inside information, embarked on a mad scramble up and down the eastern seaboard to purchase government bonds from hapless and unsuspecting war veterans at prices as low as 10 percent of full value. As Claude Bowers described in *Jefferson and Hamilton*, "[E]xpresses with very large sums of money on their way to North Carolina for purposes of speculation in certificates splashed and bumped over the wretched winter roads. . . . Two fast-sailing vessels, chartered by a member of Congress who had been an officer in the war, were ploughing the waters southward on a similar mission."[7] John Quincy Adams would later write to his father of how "Christopher Gore, the richest lawyer in Massachusetts, and one of the strongest Bay State members of Hamilton's [political] machine, had made an independent fortune in speculation in the public funds."[8]

War bonds that war veterans had "held for years" were "coaxed from them for five, and even as low as two, shillings on the pound by speculators, including the leading members of Congress, who knew that provision for the redemption of the paper [at full value] had been made," Bowers wrote.[9] "Everywhere men with capital . . . were feverishly pushing their advantage by preying on the ignorance of the poor."[10] New York newspapers speculated that Robert Morris stood to make $18 million (more than $300 million in today's dollars), while Governor George Clinton of New York would pocket $5 million.[11] Hamilton himself purchased some of the old bonds through buying agents in Philadelphia and New York but insisted that they were "for his brother-in-law."[12] For Hamilton, it would seem, the "blessings" of a national debt were personal.

To pay off the bondholders, the government needed a steady revenue stream. Thus it is perhaps not surprising that Hamilton relentlessly campaigned for a mechanism to ensure sufficient revenue and eliminate the risk of investing in government bonds:

higher taxes. Hamilton was as responsible as anyone for the tariffs and various excise taxes, including the notorious tax on whiskey, a carriage tax, and a national property tax (which spawned a tax revolt in Massachusetts—the Fries Rebellion). Plundering the working class with onerous taxes would supposedly "be a valuable spur to them," forcing them to work even harder, said Hamilton. This would be good for them, as Americans were too "indolent," he claimed.[13]

Hamilton was no "supply-sider," to use the language of modern economics. One of the tenets of supply-side economics is that it is higher *wages*—as a result of income tax *cuts,* for example—that lead to greater work effort. Faced with higher taxes, workers will have to work harder just to maintain their standard of living, or they will simply work less, since the rewards to work have been reduced. During the Reagan administration some of the liberal opponents of the supply-siders (such as the MIT economist Lester Thurow) adopted Hamilton's argument that higher taxes would be good for the economy.[14] But after the Reagan income tax cuts, the economy prospered; federal tax revenues were almost a third higher (in real, inflation-adjusted dollars) in 1990 than in 1980, since people responded to the increased rewards by working *more.*

Hamilton's plan for commandeering resources through taxation would guarantee the government a high credit rating, which would lure investors in government debt from all around the world. This was how the European empires were financed, with endless debt that was never fully paid off. If one bond issue was finally paid off, the governments would issue new bonds. The debt was never-ending. It was this very system that caused all of the European empires to bankrupt themselves, eventually.

Hamilton spent seven years attempting to overthrow the Articles of Confederation and establish a powerful central government with a new constitution, in large part so he could finance his grandiose plans. The states were able to finance the Revolution but could not be counted on to tax their citizens to support Hamilton's plans for imperial glory and national greatness. But a more powerful central government could do so, especially with a standing army of tax collectors—precisely what the response to the 1794 Whiskey Rebellion had promised. The ability to enforce such taxing and borrowing with a standing army was the most ominous aspect of the new Constitution, and it was one of the chief reasons why the Anti-Federalists never trusted Hamilton.[15] A standing army of tax collectors could (and eventually would) destroy states' rights altogether.

Hamilton's onetime political ally James Madison led the opposition to Hamilton's debt scheme and proposed to Congress that the original bondholders be paid at full value, just as the speculators were. But Hamilton's New York contingent denounced Madison "as a dreamer and an enemy of public faith," Bowers recounted, and his plan failed to pass Congress.[16] Of the sixty-four members of the House of Representatives who voted on Madison's proposal, twenty-nine were war bondholders.[17] His plan never had a chance.

Hamilton argued that a government debt fully funded by tax revenues was a form of "capital" that was literally as good as gold and would be traded on the open market as such. Such talk led the great Yale University social scientist William Graham Sumner to comment, in the early twentieth century, that Hamilton was "completely befogged in the mists of mercantilism," that his economic theories "show a remarkable amount of confusion in regard to money, capital, and debt," and that his reputation in the area of finance has "been greatly exaggerated."[18]

In reality, government borrowing *reduces* the productive capital of the private sector—the sole source of wealth creation—and diverts it to government spending programs. By shrinking the private sector in order to enlarge the state, government borrowing *harms* capital accumulation, investment, and economic growth. Hamilton had it all backward, as Sumner wrote.

Hamilton's dubious and convoluted economic arguments for debt accumulation served as a smoke screen for what Sumner called the "controlling motive": "political expediency." As Sumner noted, Hamilton himself said he wanted a large national debt because of "its tendency to strengthen our infant government by increasing the number of ligaments between the government and the interests of individuals."[19] In other words, Hamilton wanted to tie the interests of the more affluent citizens to the state. Since they would be the primary government bondholders, they would have an interest in continued borrowing and *continued tax increases* to assure that they would be paid their principal and interest. Just as today's welfare recipients are tied to government and can always be counted on to vote for its expansion, in Hamilton's day he wanted to tie *the wealthy* to the state as a permanent, big-government lobbying class.

Douglass Adair, an editor of *The Federalist Papers,* explained:

> With devious brilliance, Hamilton set out, by a program
> of class legislation, to unite the propertied interests of the
> eastern seaboard into a cohesive administration party,

while at the same time he attempted to make the executive dominant over the Congress by a lavish use of the spoils system. In carrying out his scheme . . . Hamilton transformed every financial transaction of the Treasury Department into an orgy of speculation and graft in which selected senators, congressmen, and certain of their richer constituents throughout the nation participated.[20]

This was how the Federalists became known as the "court party," the party of governmental graft, spoils, and patronage.

HAMILTON'S SECOND FINANCIAL CAPER

Hamilton prevailed in getting the central government to assume the old government debt. He then embarked on a crusade to have the central government assume the war debts of the states. He must not have thought this would be very difficult, since much of Congress had become rich from his first financial caper with regard to public debt.

During the American Revolution (and long thereafter) the colonies or states considered themselves to be free and independent. This is the exact language that was used in the Declaration of Independence. They considered themselves to be independent *countries*, just as Britain and France were independent countries. In the eighteenth century the word *congress* meant an assembly of sovereign countries. They individually taxed their citizens and borrowed as well to finance the war. When the war ended, King George III of England signed a peace treaty with each individual state, named one by one in the document, and not with some consolidated entity called "the United States government."

Consequently, each state had accumulated an amount of war debt. Some states, like Virginia, were more diligent and responsible than others, like Massachusetts, in paying off their debts. By the early 1790s Virginia had paid off most of its war debt. But at that point Hamilton proposed *socializing* or nationalizing the debt, which would force the more responsible states to pay taxes to subsidize the less responsible ones.

To fund the nationalization of the war debt, Hamilton proposed the notorious whiskey tax and other excise taxes. Jefferson and Madison opposed his plan, as did the Pennsylvanian Albert Gallatin, who would later serve as Jefferson's treasury secretary. Gallatin denounced the assumption plan as "subversive of the rights, liberty and peace of the people," and his remark was endorsed by the Pennsylvania legislature.[21] Gallatin also recognized that government debt actually drained productive investment capital from the private sector, did not "increase the existing amount of cultivated lands, of houses of consumable commodities," and did not make "the smallest addition either to the wealth or to the annual labor of a nation."[22] He understood, too, that Hamilton's tariff placed a disproportionate burden on the agricultural South, making a mockery of Hamilton's talk of "national unity" and "the common good" through big government. (Most tariffs—sales taxes on imports—were on manufactured goods and benefited mostly northern manufacturers by keeping out European competition and thereby allowing them to charge higher prices. Very little was manufactured in the agrarian South at the time, so that the tariff was all cost and no benefit to most southerners.) During the Whiskey Rebellion Hamilton tried unsuccessfully to have Gallatin arrested and put on trial.

Other critics of Hamilton's financial schemes were outraged

that a tax burden was being placed on poor farmers in order to assure interest payments to the wealthy. Still others feared that the new taxes would "let loose a swarm of harpies who, under the domination of revenue officers, will range through the country, prying into every man's house and affairs."[23] They feared, in other words, a new army of tax-collecting bureaucrats, just like the ones with whom King George III had plagued America before the Revolution.

Senator John Taylor of Virginia pointed out that consolidating taxing and borrowing powers in the central government would lead to "a suppression of the republican state assemblies, by depriving them of political importance, resulting from the imposition and dispensation of taxes."[24] This, said Taylor, would destroy the system of federalism that the Constitution created, replacing it with "a court-style English government" that would result in "the accumulation of great wealth in a few hands," accumulated through "a political moneyed engine."[25] It would create British mercantilism in America, in other words. Taylor was exactly right.

These arguments, and other criticisms by Madison, Jefferson, and others, led Congress to defeat Hamilton's assumption plan *five times,* beginning in April 1790.[26] Hamilton then used one big bargaining chip. He and his supporters wanted the nation's capital to remain in New York City; Jefferson and Madison wanted it to be located along the Potomac River in Virginia. Hamilton went to dinner with Jefferson and offered to eliminate the political opposition to moving the capital to Virginia if, in return, Jefferson (and Madison) would marshal the few congressional votes needed to get the assumption bill passed. The deal was struck; the central government assumed the state war debts; and

Washington, D.C., was created. (To secure the support of Pennsylvania's politicians, the national capital was located in Philadelphia for ten years.)

With Hamilton's Federalist Party in power, Congress's spending skyrocketed, as did taxation and governmental borrowing. Indeed, Hamilton and his fellow Federalists accumulated much more government debt than was necessary for any government expenditure programs. After all, Hamilton's objective was, first and foremost, "concentrating economic and political power in the Federal government," John C. Miller wrote in his history of the Federalist era. This would effectively abolish federalism and states' rights.[27]

Miller chronicled the results of the assumption legislation:

> [T]he national debt soared to a total of over $80 million. *To service this debt, almost 80 percent of the annual expenditures of the government were required.* During the period 1790–1800, payment of the interest alone of the national debt consumed over 40 percent of the national [tax] revenue. For a nation whose government had been tottering on the brink of bankruptcy a few years before, this might well be regarded as a staggering burden of debt.[28] (emphasis added)

The Party of Hamilton also used its power to make it illegal to criticize the government—the Federalist-controlled government, that is. With the Federalist John Adams as president, Congress passed the notorious Sedition Act, which was written so that it would expire the day Adams left office. Journalists, ordinary

citizens, and even a member of Congress—Matthew Lyon of
Vermont—were imprisoned for merely criticizing the government. A Revolutionary War veteran named Anthony Haswell,
who was the editor of the *Vermont Gazette* newspaper, was imprisoned for placing ads in Vermont newspapers requesting donations
to help pay Congressman Lyon's fines.[29] The Reverend John
C. Ogden carried a petition to Philadelphia for the release of
Congressman Lyon and was himself imprisoned for doing so. At
least twenty-one newspaper editors, *all* of whom supported Jefferson, were imprisoned. No Federalists were harassed by the Sedition Act. "Everywhere men were being intimidated into silence"
by what the historian Claude Bowers called the Federalists' "reign
of terror."[30]

Hamilton apparently did not lobby for the Sedition Act, but
he did support it once it became law. Jefferson and Madison were
again his foremost opponents, as authors of the Virginia and Kentucky Resolves of 1798, which were declarations by those two
states that they did not intend to allow the Sedition Act to be
enforced within their boundaries.[31]

Congressman Lyon enjoyed sweet revenge in 1801 when,
after being released from prison and reelected to Congress (while
still in prison), he cast the decisive vote that made Thomas Jefferson president of the United States in an election that had been
thrown into the hands of Congress.

Perhaps one of the most important aspects of Hamilton's
political legacy is that his policies led to the disintegration of the
Federalist Party. Heavy taxation, out-of-control debt, a menacing
standing army of tax collectors, and the Federalist Party's attack
on free speech led to the election of President Jefferson in 1800
and the eventual demise altogether of the Federalist Party by the

1820s. America had revolted once again against a government defined by acts of tyranny and economic exploitation. (The party died, but as we will see, its statist ideas lived on.)

President Jefferson reversed Hamilton's debt-financed spending profligacy. By 1807 his party had abolished *all* of Hamilton's excise taxes and had cut the government debt from $83 million to $57 million.[32] Jefferson adhered to his conviction that the government could borrow for such reasons as financing a defensive war, but only if the current generation was taxed to service the debt.

The Jeffersonian philosophy of government debt prevailed, more or less, for decades. Because of the War of 1812 the debt increased to $127 million by 1816, the last year of the Madison administration. Then James Monroe and John Quincy Adams reduced the debt to $58 million by 1830. President Andrew Jackson campaigned for reelection in 1832 on a platform of paying off the national debt, and he succeeded, paying off the last treasury bond in 1835. The United States was literally debt free, running a surplus, for two years. Jackson believed in the Jeffersonian dictum that government debt was dangerous to peace itself. After announcing that the government would have a positive balance of $440,000 on January 1, 1835, he said that "free from public debt," America would be "at peace with all the world. . . . The present may be hailed as the epoch in our history the most favorable for the settlement of those principles in our domestic policy which shall be best calculated to give stability to our Republic and secure the blessings of freedom to our citizens."[33]

The economic depression known as the Panic of 1837 led to an increase in deficit spending and a $16 million debt by 1845. Then President James Polk decided to start a war with Mexico in order to acquire California and other parts of that country, which drove the national debt back up to $63 million by 1848.

President Franklin Pierce, a Jeffersonian Democrat, reduced the debt back down to $28 million. With the onset of the War between the States the Lincoln administration exploded the national debt to dimensions that might have been unimaginable to Jefferson: $2.8 *billion* by 1865. But no matter how hard Lincoln tried, and how much the Republican Party was inspired by Hamiltonian economics, Republicans could not snuff out the Jeffersonian mentality among the American people. Postwar presidents such as Grover Cleveland, who vetoed more than four hundred spending bills—more than all of his predecessors combined— succeeded in whittling down the debt from $2.8 billion to $1.2 billion by the turn of the century.

It was Woodrow Wilson, whose philosophy of government was the opposite of Jefferson's in so many ways, who abandoned once and for all the Jeffersonian opposition to deficit spending and ballooned the debt to $26 billion. A case can be made that Wilson would not have been able to plunge America into the disastrous First World War without the "magic" of massive governmental debt.

The Coolidge, Harding, and Hoover administrations increased the national debt modestly, but FDR exploded it again, to $260 billion by 1945. Despite years of massive deficit spending, FDR's New Deal not only did not end the Great Depression; it actually made it worse and longer lasting. Draining billions of dollars from the private sector for the sake of expanding the government was a major reason why. The private sector is the sole source of production and wealth creation; government produces nothing at all.[34] Expanding government by shrinking the private sector is a perfect recipe for economic stagnation and depression.

The year 1960 was the last year in which the national debt actually declined. Hamiltonianism has prevailed ever since, due mostly to the efforts and legacies of big-government presidents like Lincoln, Wilson, FDR, Johnson, and George W. Bush.

A CURSED LEGACY

Perpetual government debt—as opposed to the mere emergency borrowing that Jefferson acquiesced in—essentially relies on forced labor. Citizens are forced to work to pay taxes to pay off the principal and interest on the debt. Not only are today's citizens turned into tax serfs by a large national debt, but so are future generations, who are of course politically defenseless. This is why a "good bond rating"—whether it is for bonds issued by federal or by state and local governments—does not necessarily denote a healthy economy, but merely the willingness of a governmental jurisdiction to enslave its taxpaying citizens.

To make matters worse for the average citizen, governments have historically "paid off" their debt by creating inflation with a central bank that can print money, just as any counterfeiter would. (A central bank was Hamilton's third financial caper, to be discussed in the next chapter.) Inflation constitutes a hidden tax in that it reduces the value of all privately held wealth. It is also a source of economic stagnation and political conflict, as will be discussed in more detail in the next chapter.

It is also worth noting the stark differences between private and governmental debt. When an individual borrows money, he is

obligated to pay it back. If he fails to do so, he can be held financially responsible by the legal system. And the market system
comes into play as well: individuals and businesses that renege on
their debts will become less creditworthy (or totally uncreditwor-
thy) and will have to either face higher costs of future borrowing
or forgo borrowing altogether.

Politicians, on the other hand, have no *personal* obligation
to pay anyone anything when they vote to spend more than the
tax revenues that are available. They are spending other people's
money and face little or no consequence if they spend it foolishly.
In fact, they are *rewarded* by their financial profligacy and irresponsibility: they make themselves popular by spending money
today on programs that benefit their constituents, while the bill—
paid almost exclusively by someone else—comes due much later,
perhaps even after they are retired (or dead).

Debt finance also makes it easier to devote more and more
of the taxpayers' money to special-interest politics, as opposed to
things that might conceivably benefit at least the majority of the
public. With tax finance, politicians at least have to present a case
before the voters as to why they need to pay more taxes. In doing
so they need to convince the voters that what is being proposed
will somehow benefit them and not just some special interests.
With deficit or debt finance, no such case even needs to be made
to the voters. It's spend now, pay later—much later.

Thus debt finance not only corrupts politicians; but also corrupts the voters, who become complicit in a grand scheme to stick
future taxpayers with the bill.

There is an even more insidious effect of government debt, as
the economist Hans-Hermann Hoppe explains: "[W]ith the expec-
tation of a higher future tax burden [to pay off today's governmental

borrowing], the . . . public also becomes affected by the incubus of rising time-preference degrees, for with higher future tax-rates, present consumption and short-term investment are rendered relatively more attractive as compared to saving and long-term investment."[35]

"Rising time preference" is the language economists use to describe preferences for spending more of one's income now as opposed to saving more at the present time and spending more later. A high rate of time preference denotes a penchant for being more present-oriented and for saving less. Each individual has his or her own rate of time preference, although government policy can cause shifts in these preferences, as Hoppe describes: if individuals anticipate higher taxes in the future, they will be encouraged to consume more now. Government policy can affect the rate of time preference of investors as well as consumers. If investors expect higher taxes to come, they will invest in shorter-term investments (before the tax increases take effect).

The problem here is that saving and investment are necessary for economic growth to occur. The economy cannot grow in the future if there is no capital investment today. By reducing the amount of private capital investment, governmental borrowing and the attendant tax increases that are used to pay off the principal and interest on the borrowing are detrimental to economic growth. The entire nation becomes poorer.

HAMILTONIAN VOODOO ECONOMICS

With the exception of the War between the States and the Spanish-American War periods, the Jeffersonian view of government debt (which was also Adam Smith's view) prevailed into the twentieth century. But beginning in the 1930s it was repudiated by the economics profession, particularly the followers of the British economist John Maynard Keynes.

Writing during the Great Depression, Keynes made the case that debt-financed government spending could, after all, stimulate the economy and end the depression. Since he was a distinguished Cambridge University professor, governments all around the world, including the U.S. government, used his theory to justify deficit spending. It didn't work, of course. The Roosevelt administration spent record amounts and amassed record deficits between 1933 and the U.S. entry into World War II in 1941, but it failed to end the Great Depression in America. The unemployment rate was still in double digits (14.6 percent in 1940) on the eve of the war, whereas it had been about 3.2 percent prior to the onset of the depression in 1929.

Such realities exposed the glaring inadequacies of Keynes's theory. Keynesians argued that fiscal irresponsibility on the part of government was not subject to the same principles as similar behavior on the part of individuals or families. Of course, nearly two centuries earlier Adam Smith had written that just as a family that spends more than it earns, year in and year out, will end up in bankruptcy, so will a government. Smith's view was essentially the Jeffersonian view of government debt.

Despite the obvious problems with Keynes's neo-Hamiltonian arguments, politicians welcomed Keynesian theory, which would be widely accepted for some forty years. According to Keynesians, the political class could, in effect, give the public something for nothing. All the government needed to do was to finance spending with borrowing. Government debt did not transfer the costs of government to the future, Keynesians argued, because "we owe it (the debt) to ourselves." This slogan was repeated endlessly in economics textbooks, in politicians' speeches, and on editorial pages, and it became part of the accepted public dogma with regard to government debt. But it was always nonsense.

The implication of this neo-Hamiltonian, mercantilist theory was sarcastically stated by the Nobel laureate economist James M. Buchanan and Richard E. Wagner in their book, *Democracy in Deficit:* "[T]he benefits of public spending are *always* available without cost merely by resort to borrowing. . . . If there is no transfer of cost onto taxpayers in future periods . . . there is no cost to anyone in society at the time public spending is carried out. Only the benefits of such spending remain. The economic analogue to the perpetual motion machine would have been found" (emphasis added).[36]

The result of the Keynesians' resuscitation of the Hamiltonian worship of government debt, Buchanan and Wagner continued, was that "after 1964, the United States embarked on a course of fiscal irresponsibility matched by no other period in its two-century history."[37] The year 1964 is significant because it was during the Kennedy administration that Keynesian economists achieved their greatest influence. Once the "old fiscal religion" of Jefferson and Adam Smith was forgotten, there was literally nothing—certainly not the U.S. Constitution—that restrained politicians from spending billions more than the federal treasury could afford year in and year out, creating the Leviathan State and the "empire of debt" under which Americans now slave.[38]

CHAPTER 3

∼

Hamilton's Bank Job

[A] national bank . . . was not essential to the work of the Federal Government. . . . This was . . . only a measure for carrying out the . . . interweaving of the interests of wealthy men with those of the government.

—WILLIAM GRAHAM SUMNER,
ALEXANDER HAMILTON

The Reports on Public Credit and the Bank of the United States laid the foundations for Hamilton's grand design—the centralization of governmental authority and the industrialization of the United States by means of government aid to business.

—JOHN C. MILLER, *THE FEDERALIST ERA*

The third leg of Hamilton's mercantilist stool—in addition to national debt and debt assumption—was a nationalized bank that would be managed by politicians in the nation's capital (even if ostensibly privately owned). He authored another long-winded report on the supposed constitutionality of the bank, a report that Jefferson believed was, like the others, intentionally confusing.[1] As with the national debt, the main purpose of the bank was to centralize and enlarge the state. Private banks were already in existence, and a government bank would only crowd them out and hinder their further growth. But it would also provide infinite patronage opportunities for the politicians who controlled it, just as the Bank of England had done for generations. Indeed, Hamilton's entire economic plan—of debt, a government bank, corporate welfare, heavy taxation, and a centralized state—was nothing much more than his attempt to clone the British governmental system of centralized governmental power linked to mercantilism.

James Madison was Hamilton's foremost opponent on the national bank, along with two Jeffersonians, William Giles of Virginia and James Jackson of Georgia. Jackson, like John Taylor, was shocked at the boldness of Hamilton and his party in attempting to adopt the very kind of governmental system the Revolution was fought to discard. Upon observing the corruption of Hamilton's governmental debt schemes, and hearing of his plan for a monopolistic, government-run bank, he asked, "What was it [that] drove our forefathers to this country? Was it not the ecclesiastical corps and perpetual monopolies of England and Scotland? Shall we suffer the same evils in this country?"[2]

Aside from opponents like Jackson and Madison, Hamilton faced a major hurdle: nothing in the Constitution gave the government the power to incorporate a national bank. President Washington asked his secretary of state, Jefferson, and his attorney general, Edmund Randolph, for their opinions. Both men judged the bank to be unconstitutional. Jefferson went through all the enumerated powers of Congress in Article I, Section 8, of the Constitution and found no language that would allow such an enterprise. He then examined two general phrases in Article I— the General Welfare Clause and the "Necessary and Proper"

Clause. He considered the General Welfare Clause to be, not a license for Congress to do anything it pleased, but only a reason for giving Congress certain powers of taxation. He also pointed out that the Constitutional Convention had considered giving Congress the right to establish a national bank and rejected it (based on information from James Madison, no doubt).[3]

The "Necessary and Proper" Clause says that Congress is empowered "[t]o make all Laws which shall be necessary and proper for carrying into Execution the foregoing [enumerated] Powers." All of these things can be (and had been) carried out without a nationalized bank, Jefferson argued, so the bank was unnecessary and unconstitutional. Such a bank might be "convenient" as a depository for tax revenues, he said, but it was hardly necessary. Private banks were already performing that and all other banking functions that Hamilton wanted his government-run (and -subsidized) bank to perform.

This was the essence of Jefferson's strict constructionist view of the Constitution. Madison had earlier been in favor of a more expansive interpretation of the Constitution, but on the question of the bank he accepted Jefferson's position and used his arguments in Congress to oppose the bank. Apparently Hamilton's wild and dangerous schemes persuaded Madison that not taking a strict approach to the Constitution had been mistaken.

President Washington asked Hamilton to respond to Randolph and Jefferson. He did—with 15,000 words; this was his *Opinion as to the Constitutionality of the Bank of the United States.* The crux of his opinion was that Jefferson did not understand the meaning of the word *necessary.* Although *Webster's Dictionary* defines the word as meaning "essential," "indispensable," "inevitable," and "required," Hamilton argued that it is "a matter of opinion." The powers enumerated in the Constitution ought to be construed "on principles of liberal construction," he said, "in advancement of the public good."[4] This would require giving politicians like himself "great latitude of discretion" in deciding the limits of federal governmental powers.[5] In other words, such powers should be made up, even fabricated, on the whims of politicians posing as guardians of "the public good."

He went on to say that any act of government is to be permitted if it is not expressly prohibited in the Constitution, something that he somehow forgot to mention in *The Federalist Papers,* and a notion that would have been foreign to James Madison's ears. It is unimaginable that the Constitution would ever have been adopted had it included this proposition—that the federal government possessed all powers not explicitly prohibited by the document.[6] Next he passed off his invented notion of the Constitution's "implied powers," as discussed in the previous chapter. These are powers of the central government that are not in the Constitution, and that neither the Constitutional Convention nor the state ratifying conventions considered. They are powers of government that were simply made up by politicians and judges who preferred a larger and more intrusive state. Like a national bank, for example.

President Washington signed the legislation creating the First Bank of the United States in 1791 after a compromise was reached that would enlarge the area of the District of Columbia by three miles so that it would be adjacent to his (Washington's) property along the Potomac River. Federalist senators had blocked Washington's request until he agreed to sign the bank bill.

The Bank of the United States (BUS) was given a twenty-year renewable charter. It was mostly privately owned, with the government controlling 20 percent of the shares. The bank would be the depository of government funds and would issue paper money that was backed by gold and silver.

Like all government-operated banks, the BUS quickly created inflation by printing excessive amounts of money and facilitating the state's borrowing and spending. As the economist Murray Rothbard explained in his *History of Money and Banking in the United States:*

> The Bank of the United States promptly fulfilled its inflationary potential by issuing millions of dollars in paper money and demand deposits [i.e., checking accounts], pyramiding on top of $2 million in specie [gold and silver]. The Bank . . . invested heavily in loans to the United States government. In addition to $2 million invested in the assumption of pre-existing long-term debt assumed by the new federal government, the Bank . . . engaged in massive temporary lending to the government, which reached $6.2 million by 1796. The result of the outpouring of credit and paper money by the new Bank of the United States was . . . an increase [in prices] of 72 percent [from 1791 to 1796].[7]

Northern merchants supported the BUS enthusiastically, since it extended cheap credit to many of them. Southern members of Congress were almost unanimously opposed to it, for they saw little or no benefit in it for their region and feared its potentially corrupting influence on politics. And the same class of speculators that benefited from the original national debt issues continued to benefit as the BUS was used to "monetize" even more debt, backed up by the Federalist Party's growing tax burden on the American public.

JEFFERSON PREVAILS . . . FOR A WHILE

The bank's activities brought renewed questions about its constitutionality, and Congress allowed its charter to lapse in 1811. Jefferson must have been smiling. But then the financial chaos caused by the War of 1812 led to its resurrection in the form of the Second Bank of the United States in 1817. President Madison himself supported the bank since he was then among those responsible for paying for the war (and for the rest of the government).

As soon as Hamilton's bank was revived, it "ran into grave difficulties through mismanagement, speculation, and fraud," wrote James J. Kilpatrick.[8] Such problems are, of course, characteristic of *all* governmental enterprises, especially banks. (The writer P. J. O'Rourke was only half kidding when he once wrote that giving money and power to politicians is like giving whiskey and car keys to teenage boys.) The BUS had created several regional branches, so all of this mismanagement and fraud became close to the people; it wasn't just a story about governmental antics in the faraway nation's capital. Consequently, "a wave of hostility toward the Bank of the United States swept the country," wrote Kilpatrick.[9] Indiana and Illinois, in 1816 and 1818 respectively, amended their state constitutions to prohibit the BUS from operating there.[10] North Carolina, Georgia, Maryland, Tennessee, and Kentucky imposed heavy taxes on BUS branches ($60,000 per year in Kentucky). Their purpose was to tax the bank out of existence.

The federal government brought suit in Maryland and was confident that Chief Justice John Marshall, a former protégé of Hamilton's and the keeper of the Hamiltonian flame in legal circles, would rule in its favor. He did, in the case of *McCulloch v. Maryland*, repeating almost verbatim Hamilton's arguments about the supposed "implied powers" of the Constitution. "The power to tax involves the power to destroy," he declared. And the states were attempting to destroy a federal bureaucracy that they believed was unconstitutional, and not acting in their best interest. Marshall declared the bank to be constitutional, using Hamilton's arguments about implied powers and his fanciful interpretation of the word *necessary*.

Marshall went further by asserting the false argument that the citizens of the states were never sovereign and that therefore they must always yield to the "supremacy" of the federal government. And if there were questions over how to define that supremacy, said Marshall, the job of resolving them would belong to the Supreme Court—that is, to John Marshall.

But in the early nineteenth century (and beyond, until 1865) the Supreme Court's opinion was just the Supreme Court's opinion, nothing more. Justices were not the black-robed deities that they are today. The citizens of the states took notice of Marshall's opinion and then proceeded to ignore it. Kilpatrick cites the case of Ohio in his book *The Sovereign States*. The state levied a $50,000-per-year tax on each of the BUS's two branches in the state. The BUS refused to pay, so Ohio's state auditor sent a deputy, John L. Harper, "to collect the tax by persuasion if he could, but by violence if he must."[11] When Harper was denied payment by the bank's management, he "leaped over the counter, strode into the bank vaults, and helped himself to $100,000 in paper and specie. He then turned this over to a deputy . . . stuffing this considerable hoard into a small trunk, with which he had thoughtfully come equipped."[12]

The BUS sued the deputies and the state of Ohio, relying on Marshall's imperious opinion about the federal government's supposed supremacy. The Ohio state legislature responded by thumbing its nose at the entire federal government with the following declaration:

> [We] are aware of the doctrine, that the Federal courts are exclusively vested with jurisdiction to declare, in the last resort, the true interpretation of the Constitution of the United States. To this doctrine . . . [we] can never give [our] assent.[13]

The Ohio legislature then quoted Jefferson and Madison's Virginia and Kentucky Resolves of 1798 to remind the central government that it is the people of the states who are sovereign, despite the ruminations of a single government lawyer with lifetime tenure. "The people themselves" are "the true source of all legitimate powers," the state legislature declared.[14] In the next seven or eight years Kentucky, Tennessee, Connecticut, South Carolina, New York, and New Hampshire all adopted some or all of Ohio's tactics to harass the BUS, despite Marshall's opinion in *McCulloch v. Maryland.* Yes, such a thing as "judicial review" of the constitutionality of federal legislation existed. But until the end of the War between the States, it was considered by many Americans to be merely the opinion of the Supreme Court and did not necessarily carry more weight than the opinions of the president, the Congress, or the citizens of the sovereign states.

HAMILTON'S GHOST: THIRTY YEARS OF FINANCIAL CORRUPTION AND INSTABILITY

The BUS immediately gave itself regulatory powers over other state-chartered banks. In an 1810 "memorial" to itself, the bank's directors praised themselves with a declaration that said the bank had been "a general guardian of commercial credit, and by preventing the balance of trade in the different states from producing a deficiency of money in any, has obviated the mischiefs which would have been thereby produced. It has fostered and protected the banking institutions of the States, and has aided them when unexpectedly pressed."[15]

The BUS did indeed influence the state banks, but its influence was not as benevolent as the self-serving bank directors claimed. Even when the BUS was out of business—from 1811 to 1816—the federal government maintained a regulatory role. It also encouraged the creation of more state banks during the War of 1812, since state banks could print money and purchase the federal government's war bonds. Dozens of banks became overextended, lending far more than they had in specie reserves.

Just how the BUS came to have a regulatory role over private, commercial banks chartered by the states is explained by the historian Robert Remini:

> The BUS had a powerful lever on state banks, which it achieved by acquiring their notes. This acquisition took two principal forms: since the BUS managed . . . the federal tax revenues deposited with it and since these taxes were frequently offered in the form of state bank notes, the Bank could either accept and hold the notes or it

could present them to the issuing banks and demand specie; further, since the BUS had tremendous resources of its own, it could go into the money market and buy state bank notes and then present them for redemption to the issuing banks.[16]

The success of the commercial banks depended upon their keeping their banknotes in circulation. The BUS could therefore hurt the banks' bottom line by demanding specie payment for its notes, effectively orchestrating a run on the banks. Thus, from the very beginning, government-run banking tended to control and displace private banks. While some state-chartered banks did support the BUS, they tended to do so in return for the bank's favoritism; a state-chartered bank, after all, would benefit if the BUS demanded specie payment for the notes of the state bank's *competitors*.

The federal government made a fateful decision in 1814: it allowed the state banks to suspend specie payment. That is, they were no longer required to hold sufficient gold and silver in their vaults to cover their loans, so they could lend even more to the federal government. This went on for two and a half years. The predictable effect was price inflation of as much as 55 percent per year in some cities.[17]

The creation of the Second Bank of the United States in January 1817 caused an even further expansion of bank credit (and inflation). By 1818 the BUS had lent $23 million with a specie reserve of only $2.3 million.[18] All of this cheap credit created an economic boom and fostered a great deal of real estate speculation that sharply raised property values around the country. But the BUS soon began to lose credibility, as it often failed to pay depositors in specie when they requested it. People became suspicious and alarmed at holding only pieces of paper with politicians' pictures on it as opposed to gold and silver. The bank spent huge sums purchasing specie from abroad, but that failed to stem its problems.[19]

"Beginning in the summer of 1818," Rothbard wrote, the BUS "precipitated the Panic of 1819 [the first economic depression in the new country] by a series of deflationary moves [which] . . . sharply limited and contracted the loans and note issues of the [Bank's] branches."[20] This in turn forced the state banks to reduce their loans, and the overall monetary contraction "led to a wave of bankruptcies throughout the country."[21] The real estate bubble burst, as prices overall fell precipitously. By 1819 the price of agricultural exports was less than half of what it had been a year earlier. Personal bankruptcies abounded, especially among farmers who had accumulated large amounts of debt, merchants whose retail prices fell precipitously, and land speculators.

Money was so scarce that large portions of the population resorted to bartering instead of using money. For the first time, there was large-scale unemployment in the cities. In Philadelphia, for example, manufacturing (mostly handicrafts) employment fell from 9,700 employed persons in 1815 to only 2,100 in 1819.[22] The economic depression lasted until 1821.

The Panic of 1819 was the first boom-and-bust cycle of the economy caused by government monetary policy. It was an inevitable consequence, in other words, of the Hamiltonian system of governmental debt accumulation combined with a government-run bank that prints money in order to fund the debt. This, and the growing corruption associated with the BUS, would lead President Andrew Jackson to declare war on Hamilton's bank, a war that he eventually won.

JACKSON'S WAR ON HAMILTON'S BANK

By the 1820s Hamilton's bank had proliferated into twenty-nine branches, and its main headquarters in Philadelphia had been designed "to look like a Greek temple," as many of the monuments in Washington, D.C., today also appear to be.[23] As Robert Remini wrote, the BUS "had earned widespread hatred and fear throughout a substantial part of the nation."[24]

Upon taking office in March 1829, President Jackson decried the BUS as "a monster, a hydra-headed monster . . . equipped with horns, hoofs, and tail so dangerous that it impaired the morals of our people, corrupted our statesmen, and threatened our liberty. It bought up members of Congress by the Dozen . . . subverted the electoral process, and sought to destroy our republican institutions."[25]

Liberal historians (by far the majority of the profession) have long denigrated Jackson and the Jacksonians as ignorant country bumpkins, with their party dominated by hayseed southerners like Jackson himself. But in fact the new Democratic Party of Andrew Jackson was founded primarily due to the efforts of the New Yorker Martin Van Buren, one of the most libertarian statesmen in American history. Van Buren picked up the political mantle in the mid-1820s that Jefferson himself had carried for so long. The party stood for laissez-faire in economics, a drastic reduction in tariffs, paying off the national debt (which it did), and honest money backed by gold. "Far from being the ignorant bumpkins that most historians have depicted," wrote Murray Rothbard, "the Jacksonians were steeped in the knowledge of sound economics."[26]

Rothbard went on to explain that "the Jacksonians were

libertarians. . . . They favored absolutely minimal Government. . . .
They believed that government should be confined to upholding
the rights of private property. In the monetary sphere, this meant
the separation of government from the banking system."[27] They
opposed, in other words, the objective of "energetic government"
that Hamilton championed and that generations of Hamilton-
worshipping historians have also endorsed—which might help
explain why the Jacksonians have been so incorrectly portrayed.

Whereas the Bank's main supporters, the remnants of the
old Hamiltonian political machine, came "particularly from the
upper classes," as Remini wrote, "men from all classes" and from
"every section of the country" joined President Jackson in the fight
against the BUS.[28] Jackson's treasury secretary, Roger B. Taney, the
future chief justice of the United States, publicly condemned the
Bank's "corrupting influence . . . its patronage greater than that of
the Government—its power to embarrass the operations of the
Government—and to influence elections."[29]

Nicholas Biddle, who managed the bank, did much to prove
Jackson's and Taney's points. He spent BUS funds to publish
dozens of articles in newspapers all across the country defending
the bank and attacking the Jackson administration. Biddle was, in
Remini's description, "arrogant. Impossibly arrogant. And vain . . .
There also have been questions about Biddle's integrity."[30] And
Biddle did not hesitate to use the BUS to politicize the economy.
"[H]e was not above extending the Bank's money to its friends
and refusing loans to those considered unfriendly. The favoritism
he showed toward Daniel Webster and . . . other privileged Congressmen [including Henry Clay] . . . exposed the BUS to devastating public criticism."[31]

Outraged by such behavior, Andrew Jackson also refused

to accept John Marshall's argument that the Supreme Court is necessarily the sole arbiter of questions of constitutionality. Jackson offered *his* opinion that in addition to being corrupt and a source of economic instability, the Bank was unconstitutional. Yes, the Marshall court had declared the Bank to be constitutional, but, President Jackson intoned:

> To this conclusion I cannot assent. . . . Congress and the President as well as the Court must each for itself be guided by its own opinion of the Constitution. It is as much the duty of the House of Representatives, of the Senate, and of the President to decide upon the constitutionality of any bill or resolution which may be presented. . . . The opinion of the [Supreme Court] judges has no more authority over Congress than the opinion of Congress has over the judges, and on that point the President is independent of both. The authority of the Supreme Court must not, therefore, be permitted to control the Congress or the Executive . . . but to have only such influence as the force of their reasoning may deserve.[32]

This attitude was nearly identical to the opinions of the anti-Bank state legislatures. Despite John Marshall's attempts to put *himself* in charge of interpreting the Constitution, there was widespread disagreement over the wisdom of such a judicial dictatorship.

In criticizing the bank, President Jackson also expressed a patently Jeffersonian argument about what the main purpose of government should be. No uneducated country bumpkin could have said this:

It is to be regretted that the rich and powerful too often bend the acts of government to their selfish purposes. Distinctions in society will always exist under every just government. Equality of talents, of education, or of wealth can not be produced by human institutions [but] . . . every man is equally entitled to protection by law; but when the laws undertake to add to these natural and just advantages artificial distinctions, to grant titles, gratuities, and exclusive privileges, to make the rich richer and the potent more powerful, the humble members of society . . . who have neither the time nor the means of securing like favors to themselves, have a right to complain of the injustice of their Government. . . . If [government] would confine itself to equal protection . . . it would be an unqualified blessing. In the act before me [to recharter the BUS] there seems to be a wide and unnecessary departure from these just principles.[33]

Liberal historians have denounced this classic Jeffersonian statement of the purpose of government as "beneath contempt," wrote Robert Remini. And indeed they have—and do to this day. But Andrew Jackson prevailed. While Congress voted to reinstate the BUS, he vetoed the bill, and Congress did not have the votes to override the veto. He then withdrew all government funds from the Bank, allowing it to die a quiet death several years later. But Biddle attempted one final act of revenge. He supervised a general curtailment of lending throughout the entire banking system in an attempt to create a depression, which he hoped would somehow force President Jackson to return the tax revenues to the Bank. He created a recession in parts of the country, but his one final act of political monetary manipulation failed to save the Bank. He was forced to vacate his cherished Greek temple in downtown Philadelphia.

HAMILTON'S DISASTROUS MONETARY LEGACY

After the demise of the Second Bank of the United States an alternative monetary system was adopted in which all currency was backed by specie on demand. A number of economic historians consider this so-called Independent Treasury System to have been the most stable monetary system of the nineteenth century. As we will see, however, the Hamiltonian system was revived during the Lincoln administration with the National Currency Acts, and ultimately in 1913 the creation of the Federal Reserve System instituted full-fledged central banking. Thus political control of the money supply is another important element of Hamilton's legacy.

That legacy can be described, in a nutshell, as inflation, debasement of the currency (i.e., reducing the spending power of the dollar), and perpetual economic instability through politically contrived boom-and-bust cycles in the economy.

Government control of the money supply amounts to legalized counterfeiting. The ability to print paper money is even more of a politician's dream than the ability to incur government debt, for no direct taxation is involved in the government's efforts to secure resources from the public. It all seems painless to the taxpayers—as long as they remain ignorant about the effects of inflation.

Politicians benefit from inflation by spending billions of dollars on various constituent groups and effectively buying votes (and campaign contributions). These individuals and groups may benefit from inflation because of their political connections, but as prices rise, year in and year out, most of society loses. This is especially true of anyone whose income is relatively fixed, such as people on salaries that may not keep up with inflation, retired people, and anyone holding cash assets. To all of these people, inflation is indeed a hidden tax.

In addition to being an indirect or hidden tax, inflation interferes with what economists call "economic calculation," and this harms the entire economy. If general economic growth is subsequently slower, then the entire society is "taxed" again from inflation.

Rothbard gave an example of how this works: "[A]ccounting practice enters the 'cost' of an asset [to a business] at the amount the business has paid for it. But if inflation intervenes, the cost of replacing the asset when it wears out will be far greater than that recorded on the books. As a result, business accounting will seriously overstate their profits during inflation."[34] Thus business profits are reduced by inflation. In addition, the uncertainty that is created over the true costs of running a business causes firms to become more hesitant to invest in business expansion. Calculating expected profits from an investment in a new factory or piece of equipment becomes much more difficult, if not impossible, when there is no way of knowing with any certainty what the future prices of the equipment or of the products produced with the equipment (and wages, utility bills, etc.) will be.

Inflation encourages personal debt and discourages savings or thrift, for any amount of money that is lent will be repaid in future dollars that are of reduced value thanks to inflation. Less personal savings means less capital is available to be borrowed by businesses (and/or interest rates are pushed up). Less business investment today means less production and employment tomorrow, along with even higher prices due to the reduced supply of goods.

Inflation is also the chief cause of the boom-and-bust business cycle that is characterized by wide swings, over time, in inflation and unemployment, among other things. Governmental credit expansion increases lending to businesses, and the new money is invested in myriad projects and is paid out to workers and others. But the level of investment will be artificially high. That is, businesses will invest more than they would if their investment were based primarily on the free-market decisions of individuals to save and invest—on consumers' ability to purchase the products that are eventually produced by all the investment. Eventually, then, many investments are deemed to be wasteful and have to be liquidated. This is what constitutes the "bust" part of the business cycle, otherwise known as a recession or a depression.

It was the "easy money" policies of the late 1920s, for example, that spawned the Great Depression, less than twenty years after the creation of the Federal Reserve System.[35] Americans have endured periodic boom-and-bust cycles ever since. To make matters worse, government uses the economic chaos created by government-manufactured boom-and-bust cycles as a justification for adopting even more socialistic central planning of the economy. Such planning inevitably backfires and makes things even worse, thanks to the economic "law of unintended consequences." Then government uses *that* as an excuse to give itself even *more* central planning powers, and on and on the charade goes. The economy becomes more and more disabled while more and more individual liberty disappears.

America's economic history since Hamilton fought for his

centrally planned economy bears all this out. Needless to say, Hamilton never hinted that such problems could result from his plans. But his critics at the time, even without the benefit of a formal economic theory to explain the causes of the boom-and-bust cycle, voiced exactly such concerns. They knew from intuition and experience the dangers that Hamilton's scheme promised to bring.

POLITICAL CONTROL

It is remarkable that a man like Hamilton, who is considered to have been as politically astute as anyone of his day, could get away with *any* "public interest" arguments—for a national bank, national debt, or anything else. The reason is simple: *The Federalist Papers*, of which he was one of the principal authors, had argued repeatedly, and correctly, that politicians can never be trusted to behave "in the public interest," however it may be defined. They may do so on occasion, but in general they behave *in their own self-interests*, which are in the public's best interest only by accident. "If men were angels," Madison famously announced, there would be no need for government at all. In other words, if politicians really did behave selflessly, and acted only "in the public interest," they would be more like angels than human beings. That is why government needed to be bound by a constitution, said the founders.

Hamilton endorsed all of this thinking as coauthor of *The Federalist Papers*. But then he immediately went about repudiating those arguments, day in and day out, as he campaigned for nationalized banking and debt and many other forms of government intervention, all based on the illogical notion that political "angels" (in the form of Federalist politicians) could indeed be found to manage these governmental institutions "in the public interest."

It is no surprise that the Bank of the United States almost immediately destabilized the economy and made political mischief by, for example, using of Bank funds—taxpayer funds—to attempt to influence elections. As the late Nobel laureate economist Milton Friedman once said, a government institution that is not dominated by politics is as likely as a barking cat.

Hamilton surely must have understood this. He wanted a government-controlled national bank precisely because he favored much more political control of society. The results have not been surprising, but they have nonetheless been devastating.

CHAPTER 4

~

Hamilton's Disciple:
How John Marshall
Subverted the Constitution

[M]any of the great Supreme Court decisions [that Chief Justice John Marshall] handed down were based on concepts articulated by Hamilton.
　　　—RON CHERNOW, *ALEXANDER HAMILTON*

If John Marshall was the father of judicial review, Hamilton was the grandfather. . . . He deserves a statue in front of the Supreme Court.
　　　—RICHARD BROOKHISER,
　　　ALEXANDER HAMILTON: AMERICAN

John Marshall was appointed chief justice of the United States by President John Adams and served in that capacity from March 3, 1801, until his death in 1835. He was a political compatriot of Hamilton's (also serving as secretary of state under President Adams). Marshall, in fact, "revered Hamilton," as the Hamilton biographer Ron Chernow noted, "having once observed that next to the former treasury secretary he felt like a mere candle 'beside the sun at noonday.'"[1]

The worshipful chief justice was also an extreme devotee of Hamilton's nationalism and statism. When Hamilton and the Federalists failed to create a "national" government at the Constitutional Convention, their strategy shifted to one of *subverting* the "frail and worthless fabric" of the Constitution through the judicial system. For example, Federalist judges—who had a near monopoly in federal judgeships in the Washington and Adams administrations—enforced the insidious Sedition Act, which was a blatant attack on the First Amendment guarantee of free speech. Their purpose in enforcing this act (exclusively against members of the opposition party) was neither justice nor national security but to protect and expand the power of the Federalist Party.

The reason President John Adams appointed dozens of "midnight judges" to the federal judiciary shortly before leaving office was to ensure that the party faithful could continue to effectively rewrite (and subvert) the *federal* system of government that was created by the Constitution. His biggest "success" in this regard was the appointment of John Marshall to the Supreme Court. As we shall see, many of Marshall's most important decisions were almost verbatim copies of Hamilton's own arguments.

Marshall rarely, if ever, relied on information from the Constitutional Convention itself, or on the state ratification conventions, in his constitutional interpretations. Instead, he cited *The Federalist Papers*, which were predominantly the Hamiltonians' nationalist views of what the Constitution *should* look like—views that had been *rejected* by the convention. He worked diligently for thirty-five years to replace the Constitution with "constitutional law," which is very different from and often has nothing in common with the actual Constitution. Marshall's "constitutional law" went a long way toward helping the Hamiltonian nationalists surreptitiously alter the form of government in America from Jeffersonian federalism to Hamiltonian nationalism and governmental consolidation.

THE GENESIS OF AMERICA'S "JUDICIAL DICTATORSHIP"

Common sense suggests that it would have been the height of absurdity for the Founding Fathers to fight a revolution in the name of liberty and then turn around and write a constitution that placed *everyone's* liberty in the hands of five government lawyers with lifetime tenure. Even more irrational would be the notion of allowing the central government to be the sole arbiter of the limits of its own powers by granting it the sole right to interpret the constitutionality of legislation through its own court system. Surely it would sooner or later decide that *there are no limits* to its powers. This was a fear often expressed by the Jeffersonians. In his book *Tyranny Unmasked*, John Taylor wrote, for example, that since constitutional government was "an essential principle for preserving liberty," the Constitution "never could have designed to destroy it [liberty], by investing five or six men [Supreme Court justices], installed for life, with a power of regulating the constitutional rights of all political departments."[2]

Another Virginian, St. George Tucker, expressed a similar opinion in his *View of the Constitution of the United States*, a book that, during the early nineteenth century, was considered to be an expression of the Jeffersonian interpretation of the Constitution. Tucker taught law at William and Mary College, was the adoptive father of John Randolph of Roanoke, and authored one of the very first plans for the peaceful abolition of slavery in 1796. In his book

he wrote that if the "unlimited authority" of the central government were ever to extend so far as to change the Constitution
itself through judicial fiat, then "the government, whatever be its
form," would become "absolute and despotic."[3]

Yet that is exactly where America stands today, and no one is
more responsible for this state of affairs than Chief Justice John
Marshall, the original champion of the Hamiltonian interpretation of the Constitution. Americans are truly living in "Hamilton's
country" (of lawyers).

Marshall did not waste any time in his crusade to turn the
federalist Constitution into a nationalist document. His first
opportunity came shortly after his first cousin, Jefferson, was inaugurated as president in March 1801. One of Adams's "midnight
judges" was a man named William Marbury, who had been
appointed as a justice of the peace in Washington, D.C. He was
appointed, but Adams's secretary of state—none other than John
Marshall—neglected to deliver to him his actual commission, a
legal document that would grant him judicial powers. When
James Madison became secretary of state under the newly
installed President Jefferson, he had no intention of delivering
commissions to *any* of the midnight judges. Then Jefferson
announced that he considered the commissions of the forty-two
judges void. Marbury sued the government for his commission,
bringing his lawsuit directly to the U.S. Supreme Court.[4] He
wanted the Court to order Secretary of State Madison to deliver
his commission to him.

Marbury brought his suit to the Supreme Court because the
Judiciary Act of 1789 gave the Court jurisdiction in such cases.
After two years of legal wrangling the Court found that Congress
had no constitutional right to assign such jurisdiction. That part of

the Judiciary Act of 1789 was therefore unconstitutional. Marbury lost the case and did not receive his commission. Jefferson was pleased. But so was John Marshall.

Judge Andrew Napolitano explains why the scheming Marshall, who wrote the Court's opinion, must have been so pleased: "*Marbury v. Madison* is the most important court decision in American history because it created *judicial review*—the power of the Supreme Court, and eventually all federal courts, to examine a statute (and eventually the behavior of the president as well) and to declare it void if the court finds it to run counter to the Constitution."[5] This means that "the Supreme Court granted itself the authority to declare the will of the people (as represented through Congress) as null and void."[6]

Napolitano points out that "*Marbury v. Madison* put Hamilton's notions into practice."[7] This is quite true. Hamilton's preference was for a judicial dictatorship that would be dominated by nationalists like himself. He made his case in *Federalist* no. 78, writing: "A constitution is in fact, and must be, regarded as a fundamental law. It therefore belongs *to them* [that is, to courts] to ascertain its meaning as well as the meaning of any particular act proceeding from the legislative body" (emphasis added). After advocating such dictatorial powers for the federal judiciary, Hamilton went on to insist that the federal judiciary would be a benevolent dictatorship that would act only in the public interest. He argued that the judiciary "will always be the least dangerous to the political rights of the Constitution"; that it would be "the weakest of the three departments of power"; that "the general liberty of the people can never be endangered" by federal judges; and that there would never be a "superiority of the judicial to the legislative power." It's safe to say that history has proven all of these promises to be false.

In *Marbury v. Madison* John Marshall essentially asserted that *he*, as chief justice, had power over *all* congressional legislation. A government lawyer with lifetime tenure, who never had to face an election or even respond to public criticism, would decide for everyone what the Constitution *really* meant. He would do so under Alexander Hamilton's preferred "expansive" view of the Constitution, reinterpreting the document so as to enlarge the state as much as possible.

Then again, as mentioned in Chapter 3, just because John Marshall offered this opinion did not mean that all Americans accepted it. Jefferson expressed his own view clearly in a September 6, 1819, letter to Judge Spencer Roane: "My construction of the constitution is . . . that each department [i.e., branch of government] is truly independent of the others, and has an *equal right* to decide for itself what is the meaning of the constitution in the cases submitted to its action" (emphasis added).[8] Many other Americans shared this view, which is why numerous state legislatures, and presidents, considered their opinions to be just as important as the Court's. For example, in the showdown over the Bank of the United States, decades after *Marbury v. Madison* was decided, northern and southern states invoked the Jeffersonian philosophy of nullification to ignore federal laws that they believed were unconstitutional. Likewise, northern states ignored President Madison's trade embargo and refused to participate in the War of 1812, while southern states nullified the hated 1828 "Tariff of Abominations."

Not until the 1860s did the power of the Supreme Court to

decide the constitutionality of federal legislation become more or less supreme. As Woodrow Wilson correctly observed in a book written while he was still a Princeton University professor, "The War between the States established . . . this principle, that the federal government is, through its courts, the final judge of its own powers."[9] The question of federal judicial supremacy was a matter of legal and political debate until the Hamiltonian position was backed up with the full military might of the U.S. government—until, that is, the debate was ended literally at gunpoint.

THE "LEAST DANGEROUS" BRANCH?

In *The Federalist Papers* Alexander Hamilton had assured Americans that the judiciary "will always be the least dangerous to the political rights of the Constitution." But his disciple John Marshall, not content with declaring federal judges with lifetime tenure "supreme" over the elected representatives of Congress, revealed the emptiness of that assurance in subsequent moves. In a series of cases Marshall and his like-minded (nationalist) Supreme Court colleagues asserted the Court's alleged supremacy over both state legislatures and state courts. Here he was furthering another of Hamilton's political goals: the political neutering of the states in the federal system.

The Constitutional Convention had rejected the notion that the federal government should have veto power over state courts. Drawing on *The Documentary History of the Ratification of the Constitution,* the constitutional historian Kevin R. C. Gutzman writes of how the Constitutional Convention denied Congress the power to veto acts of state legislatures, and it "certainly did not mean such power to be assumed by the Court instead."[10] Gutzman notes that, during the Virginia ratifying convention, some extremely intelligent and educated people labored over every detail of the document for weeks, with an eye to possible infringements of states' rights.

John Taylor also documented this point in *New Views of the Constitution of the United States*, published in 1823 and based on the notes on the Constitutional Convention taken by Robert Yates. "The proposals for a national government and its negative power over the state acts, were really made" at the Constitutional Convention, Taylor wrote. But "they were opposed by the state deputies" and "they were rejected."[11] The states were sovereign, after all.

Marshall attempted to reverse this understanding in an 1810 case known as *Fletcher v. Peck*.[12] This case involved a bribery scandal in which a group of "investors" bribed almost the entire Georgia legislature into selling them an enormous amount of land—most of what is now Alabama and Mississippi—for next to nothing. The fraudulent sale was repealed by a state law, and the corrupt legislators were all turned out of office.

Marshall, writing for the Court, declared that the Georgia law violated the Contract Clause of the Constitution, because the land sale had been secured with a binding contract and therefore could not be invalidated. This was an astounding decision, for it was widely understood at the time that in order for a contract to be valid there must not be fraud. But in the case of the Georgia land sale there certainly was fraud, and everyone knew it. This left the citizens of Georgia with no remedy for their blatantly corrupt and criminal legislature.

This didn't seem to matter to Marshall, who was himself a large land investor. What mattered was to establish the precedent—mentioned nowhere in the Constitution and explicitly rejected by the Constitutional Convention—that the federal courts could review and veto state as well as federal legislation. Hamilton's dream of a "permanent president" may have been lost, but a federal judicial dictatorship—operated by political compatriots like John Marshall—would probably have satisfied him.

This, too, was not universally accepted at the time. Unlike contemporary Americans, early-nineteenth-century Americans did not cower at the sight and pronouncements of their "supreme" judicial rulers.

It wasn't only the state legislatures that were capable of expressing the will of the citizens of the states—a will that could at times conflict with the political objectives of the relatively small number of men running the central government. The state *courts* could also cause trouble for those, like Hamilton and Marshall, who sought to consolidate political power in the nation's capital.

Marshall attempted to stomp out this challenge to "federal supremacy" in an 1816 case known as *Martin v. Hunter's Lessee*.[13] In this case the state of Virginia had seized land owned by British loyalists during the Revolution. This was before the Fifth Amendment Takings Clause had been added to the Constitution. Although Virginia's state courts had ruled that the land seizure was legitimate, the U.S. Supreme Court disagreed, citing the Jay Treaty that ended the war and enabled British citizens to own land in America. Marshall's ally on the Court, fellow nationalist Joseph Story, wrote the Court's opinion. In opposing the state courts' position, Story cited the Supremacy Clause of the Constitution, which gives the central government authority over the states *only with regard to the eighteen enumerated powers in Article I, Section 8*— that is, the powers expressly delegated to it by the sovereign states.

Story ignored the Constitution itself and, like Marshall, invented a theory to the effect that the central government's "supremacy" is virtually unlimited and applies even to land inheritances.

Nothing in the Constitution gave the federal government the power to review state court decisions; Story (with the approval of Marshall) simply asserted such powers. Once again, it was not the Constitution that the justices were applying but "constitutional law." Kevin Gutzman was surely right when he wrote that "the Marshall Court, not the Virginia judiciary, was violating the Constitution. The result was not only that the Virginia courts were overruled, and the relevant Virginia laws were voided, but that the Supreme Court seized the power to supervise state courts, an entirely unconstitutional usurpation of power."[14]

MARSHALL REWRITES HISTORY

Marshall's most audacious act was to fabricate a false history of the American founding in the 1819 case of *McCulloch v. Maryland*. In this case Maryland, like Ohio and other states, had imposed a tax on a branch of the Bank of the United States. The purpose was to tax the bank out of existence—at least within the borders of the state. The Bank refused to pay, and a lawsuit was filed against the state of Maryland. (James McCulloch was an employee of the BUS.)

As the legal scholar Edward S. Corwin pointed out, it is "well known" that for his written opinion in this case, Marshall depended on Alexander Hamilton's earlier argument about the constitutionality of the BUS, which he had written on February 23, 1791.[15] As such, Marshall adopted Hamilton's fanciful definition of the word *necessary* with regard to the "Necessary and

Proper" Clause of the Constitution. He interpreted it as meaning merely "useful" or "convenient," as Hamilton had done almost two decades earlier. He further insisted that, in addition to the expressly delegated powers of the national government, there are also "implied powers." This of course was also a verbatim copy of Hamilton's opinion.

To counter the Jeffersonian strict constructionists who argued that only express powers are legitimate and, moreover, that the Tenth Amendment to the Constitution reserves all other powers for the states and the people, respectively, Marshall deployed the Hamiltonian Big Lie that the states were never sovereign and that the Constitution was somehow the result of a national plebiscite. He claimed that the Constitution was ratified by "the whole people" of the United States, not by the citizens of the independent states. "The government of the Union . . . is, emphatically, and truly, a government of the people. In form and in substance it emanates from them. Its powers are granted by them, and are to be exercised directly on them, and for their benefit."[16] If "the whole people" gave the national government its powers, he continued, then no state can interfere with the exercise of those powers, even if they are "implied" powers that are not expressly listed in Article I, Section 8, of the Constitution.

This theory, however, was "both historically incorrect and intellectually dishonest," writes Judge Napolitano.[17] All one has to do to disprove this theory is to read Article VII of the Constitution: "The Ratification of the Conventions of nine States shall be sufficient for the Establishment of this Constitution between the States so ratifying the Same."[18] The Constitution was ratified not by any national vote but by state political conventions (*not* state legislatures) composed of representatives from all the various communities within the states. Moreover, women did not have the right to vote in America until 1920, so "the whole people" could hardly have ratified the Constitution. Not to mention the fact that slaves and free blacks had no role whatsoever in politics at the time.

Marshall's (and Hamilton's) nationalist superstition about the ratification of the Constitution is patently false. But that didn't matter. Marshall had granted himself and his fellow justices the power to codify Hamiltonian nationalism. "From the grave, the practically defunct Federalist Party and its late chieftain, Alexander Hamilton, had their way," writes Kevin Gutzman. "[T]he Philadelphia Convention, the ratification process, the Tenth Amendment, and the political defeat of the Federalist Party . . . were all undone by the Marshall Court."[19]

The Marshall Court went a long way toward establishing the "invisible sovereignty" that pervades every city, town, and state in America. The federal government is always ready to reach in and nullify or veto the will of the people of the states, or to order them to obey its own dictates. "[T]he Government of the Union," Marshall himself wrote, may "legitimately control all individuals or governments within the American territory."[20] It is doubtful that any state would have ratified the Constitution had they known that it would come to this, thanks to Hamilton and his disciple John Marshall.

It would take a while, however, before these strange Hamiltonian superstitions could be enforced. As President Andrew Jackson reportedly said about another of Marshall's opinions, "Mr. Marshall has issued his opinion, now let him try and enforce it." Hamilton's political heirs (Joseph Story, Daniel Webster, Henry Clay, and Abraham Lincoln) would repeat this false history for the next four decades as they attempted to persuade and litigate their way toward a monopolistic and mercantilistic national government—Hamilton's dream.

The strategy of persuasion and litigation ended, as we have seen, in the 1860s. As Edward Corwin wrote in *John Marshall and the Constitution*, "[U]ntil the Civil War . . . the great mass of Americans still felt themselves to be first of all citizens of their respective States."[21] Corwin, a champion of and an apologist for Marshall's nationalistic views, never missed an opportunity to denigrate the notion of state sovereignty for its "individualistic bias"—that is, for its notion that individual rights ought to be protected by government. He smeared state sovereignty by comparing it to a "serpent" and a "dangerous enemy to national unity."[22] He rejoiced over the fact that Marshall had gone so far to destroy the "irrelevant notion of State Sovereignty."[23] He even named a chapter of his book "The Menace of States Rights."

Of course, state sovereignty was a reality—at least until it was washed away in the 1860s. The founders recognized that the only way to control the central government that the citizens of the states had created, and to make it serve as the citizens' agent rather than as their master, was through the efforts of political communities organized at the state and local levels. This is how the Constitution was to be enforced. Madison called it "dual sovereignty," also known as federalism.

Thus Hamilton and Marshall's war on state sovereignty was a war against the very notion that *the citizens* should be sovereign over their own government. "Citizen sovereignty" would be an even more accurate phrase than "state sovereignty." It is disputed whether Hamilton ever called the public "a great beast," as some historians have purported, but whether he said it or not, his behavior—and the behavior of his political disciples like John Marshall—indicates that he did hold the public in such low regard.

Observing all of this near the end of his life, Thomas Jefferson offered his opinion in a December 25, 1820, letter to Thomas Ritchie. As threatening to liberty as Congress was beginning to seem, Jefferson wrote, "it is not from this branch of government we have most to fear."[24] The real problem was that "the judiciary of the United States is the subtle corps of sappers and miners constantly working under ground to undermine the foundations of our confederated fabric. They are construing our constitution from a co-ordination of a general and special government to a general and supreme one alone."[25] (A sapper is a soldier who digs battlefield fortifications.)

Jefferson next addressed the issue of how the U.S. Senate had failed to convict the Federalist Supreme Court justice Samuel Chase after the House of Representatives had overwhelmingly impeached him for behaving in a prejudiced, partisan way in his enforcement of the Sedition Act. "Having found . . . that impeachment is an impracticable thing, a mere scare-crow," Jefferson wrote, Federalist judges like Marshall "consider themselves secure for life; they sculk from responsibility to public opinion, the only remaining hold on them."[26] The Court's opinions, moreover, seemed to be "huddled up in conclave, perhaps by a majority of one, delivered as if unanimous, and with the silent acquiescence of lazy or timid associates, by a crafty chief judge [Marshall], who sophisticates the law to his mind, by the turn of his own reasoning."[27]

Illustrating Jefferson's point, Marshall interpreted the Constitution as "expansively" as possible in order to enhance the power of the central government and prohibit the citizens of the independent states from exerting *their* influence. He disallowed the New Hampshire legislature from influencing the method by which Dartmouth College, a state-chartered institution that had received state government funds during the colonial era, chose its board of directors; and he invented a very broad definition of *commerce* in the 1824 case of *Gibbons v. Ogden*, a definition that would eventually open the door to federal regulation of virtually *all* business in America. In recent years, for example, federal jurists have argued that the federal government has the power to decide on gun-control policy in the vicinity of schools because it can be said to affect interstate commerce. How? Because schools are about education; education affects the productivity of the workforce; the workforce produces goods that cross state lines; therefore schools, and all the activities involved with schools, supposedly constitute "interstate commerce." Even more convoluted reasoning has been used in thousands of other cases, and it all started with John Marshall and his crusade to "write Hamiltonian principles into legal precedent," as Gutzman put it.[28]

So by the 1830s the voluntary union of the founders was falling victim to creeping consolidation, thanks to the influence of Hamilton and his political heirs. This was truly a curse on America, for it sowed the seeds of civil war. In a nation as big as the United States—even in the early nineteenth century—there were bound to be numerous powerful regional differences based primarily on economics. The agrarian South had many interests that were starkly different from those of the increasingly manufacturing-based North, for example. With a truly consolidated or monopoly government, only one of those interests could prevail at any one time. That, in turn, inevitably leads to the outcome of one section of the country using the powers of the state to plunder and exploit the other sections, all under the phony guise of "national unity." (There was forced "national unity" in the Soviet Union for decades, the reader may recall.)

This is precisely why the founders created a system of federalism, or decentralized government, and why Jefferson believed that the Tenth Amendment, which reserved the bulk of governmental powers to the states, was the most important part of the Constitution. Along with the whittling away of federalism by the Hamiltonians (also known as the Federalists, Northern Whigs, and Republicans) came increasing regional conflict and strife, ending with the War between the States.

HAMILTON'S VICTORY

In *Alexander Hamilton and the Constitution* Clinton Rossiter remarked that "Hamilton had no equal among the men who chose to interpret the Constitution as a reservoir of national energy."[29] All the Federalists, from John Jay to Rufus King to Marshall, owed Hamilton a debt of thanks for "having taught his friends how to read the Constitution," Rossiter noted. These men were probably already disposed to reading things into the Constitution that were not there, but "there is little doubt that they first learned the details of their constitutional law in the official papers of the Secretary of the Treasury."[30] It was Hamilton who taught them how to subvert the Constitution, a task they would embark upon for the rest of their lives. Senator Rufus King of Massachusetts was so impressed with Hamilton's skill at subverting the Constitution with his rhetoric that he promised him "assistance to whatever measures and maxims he would pursue."[31]

Supreme Court justice Joseph Story, appointed to the Court in 1811, "became the most Hamiltonian of judges. He construed the powers of Congress liberally; he upheld the supremacy of the nation [i.e., the central government] doggedly; he even found the Alien and Sedition Laws constitutional in retrospect."[32] Story wrote his *Commentaries on the Constitution* in 1833, which became the party line for Federalist/Whig subverters of the original Constitution with their "constitutional law." The book could have just as easily been entitled "Commentaries on Alexander Hamilton's Commentaries on the Constitution," wrote Rossiter.[33]

Story expounded the Hamiltonian superstitions of "implied" and "resultant" powers of the Constitution, championed executive power and judicial review by the federal judiciary alone, and proclaimed the "supremacy" of the central government. As Rossiter observed, this book provided a legal road map for "the legal [profession's] elite—or at least among the part of it educated in the North—during the middle years of the nineteenth century."[34] Thus this "elite" would continue the Hamilton/Marshall tradition of constitutional subversion up through the War between the States and beyond. Abraham Lincoln would repeat Hamiltonian notions of "national supremacy" and denials of state sovereignty to justify his military invasion of the southern states, even if he did not cite Hamilton per se in his speeches.

Liberal and leftist historians invariably celebrate the fact that "the principles of Hamilton have governed the development of American constitutional law since the middle of the 1930s."[35] These principles have been used to rationalize federal power grab after federal power grab, and they are the basis for the federal Leviathan State that liberals and leftists so cherish. They are the rhetorical enablers of the New Deal and its political legacies. "Not until the final victory of the New Deal," wrote Rossiter, "did the principles of nationalism and broad construction expounded by Hamilton and his disciples" finally monopolize discussion of constitutional law.[36] "We live today—and will live indefinitely . . . under a Hamiltonian Constitution."[37]

Liberals like the late Clinton Rossiter have loudly celebrated this fact in their writings. "The formula for congressional authority today [the 1960s] reads: the commerce power + the war powers + the power to tax and spend for the general welfare x the loosest possible reading of the words 'necessary and proper.' "[38] The result is "an unchallengeable authority to pass laws dealing with almost any problem that appears to be national in scope, including problems of agriculture, health, education, conservation, morals, welfare, and civil rights."[39] This sounds more like the old Soviet Constitution than the U.S. Constitution.

This formula is nothing to celebrate. It has produced a uniquely American brand of judicial and legislative totalitarianism, in which the Constitution is meaningless as a restraint on governmental power. Thanks to Hamilton, Marshall, and their ideological heirs, Americans live under a Constitution that is construed by the courts as a grant of powers and not as a restraint on government, as was originally intended. It is, Rossiter gushed, "a grant of splendid powers rather than a catalogue of niggling limitations. We go to it for support rather than admonition, for encouragement rather than dissuasion, for ways to get things done [by government] rather than to keep things from being done [by government]."[40] This of course is exactly the opposite of the original intent of the framers of the Constitution.

The president is no longer the chief administrator of a modest governmental apparatus, as George Washington was. Thanks to Hamilton's theories of executive power, as interpreted and applied by such figures as Lincoln and the two Roosevelts, American presidents have assumed "vast responsibilities at home and abroad" and consider themselves to be, more or less, the chief executives of the entire planet. (One might recall President George W. Bush announcing his goal of eliminating tyranny from the earth in his second inaugural address.)

Rossiter was certainly right when he wrote that the Hamilton/Marshall view of the Constitution prevailed with a vengeance beginning in the 1930s. *Between 1937 and 1995, not a single federal law was declared to be unconstitutional by the Supreme Court.* Not one among hundreds of decisions and thousands of pieces of legislation.[41] Hamilton had won: any legislation that is not explicitly prohibited by the Constitution is permitted. Just about anything goes, in other words. The Court paid great deference to the hyperactive legislature and no longer served as any kind of check on unconstitutional legislation. And by that time the states were also neutered, since the rights of nullification and secession were abolished in 1865. The Washington establishment has long considered the taxpayers' pockets to be an inexhaustible resource, one they can plunder with the validation of the Constitution. Nor are there any longer any serious constraints on government's ability to centrally plan, regulate, control, and regiment all businesses in America, despite its track record of providing little or no benefits from regulation while burdening the nation with billions of dollars of regulatory costs annually.[42]

As the great French economist Frédéric Bastiat once remarked, democracy can be just as oppressive as dictatorship if the results of democracy are forced uniformity.[43] What is the difference, after all, between a dictator's edict that everyone in an entire country must behave in a particular way and the exact same edict enacted and enforced by a legislature? Both are examples of coerced "national uniformity," something that statists of all stripes typically celebrate with nice-sounding words like "union" and "national unity."

Once the Court abandoned all pretense of performing its duties of seriously applying the words of the Constitution to legislation, all the federal government had to do to have any legislation pass constitutional muster was to make an argument, however weak, that the legislation in question was somehow serving "the common good," Hamilton's favorite phrase. Thus in the 1937 case of *West Coast Hotel v. Parrish* a minimum-wage law for women that had previously been ruled a violation of the Contract Clause of the Constitution suddenly became constitutional.[44] The government could pass laws that violated private wage contracts after all, "in the common good."

During that same year, in *NLRB v. Jones & Laughlin Steel Corp.*, the Court upheld the National Labor Relations Act, under which the government had given itself the right to regulate labor relations. The Court's argument was that labor relations affected interstate commerce and that therefore the Commerce Clause of the Constitution allowed for federal regulation of all labor relations. The actual case involved ten employees of U.S. Steel (out of 56,000) who had complained of being treated unfairly by the company since they were union sympathizers. The government ordered U.S. Steel to be nicer to those ten men, whose actions supposedly had an important impact on interstate commerce in America.[45] Under such twisted (Hamiltonian) logic, the government imposed minimum-wage, maximum-hour, and child-labor legislation. These were all obvious violations of freedom of contract (between employers and employees), but the Court gave Congress the right to regulate any business behavior that might conceivably affect interstate commerce. (Recall that it was Hamilton who was the first to suggest this as the "proper" interpretation of the Commerce Clause.)

Years after FDR's death his chief domestic policy adviser from 1932 to 1945, Rexford Tugwell of Columbia University, candidly admitted that these and myriad other decisions by the "Roosevelt Court" were "the tortured interpretations of a document [the Constitution] intended to prevent them."[46] Hamilton and Marshall would have been very proud.

CHAPTER 5

~

The Founding Father
of Crony Capitalism

The system of protection[ism] to be found in this report of Hamilton's is the old system of mercantilism of the English school, turned around and adjusted to the situation of the United States.

—WILLIAM GRAHAM SUMNER,
ALEXANDER HAMILTON

After Alexander Hamilton and his party were repudiated in the election of 1800, the newly elected president, Thomas Jefferson, used his inauguration to enunciate laissez-faire principles that he believed should guide America into the new century. In his first inaugural address he explained that "a wise and frugal Government" was one that protected the lives and liberties of its citizens, period. Citizens, he said, should otherwise be free to earn a living without government interference, especially heavy taxation, which would "take from the mouth of labor the bread it has earned."

Hamilton responded with a vitriolic attack in which he called Jefferson's speech a "symptom of a pygmy mind."[1] He viewed his rival's inaugural address as a direct assault on the economic theories he had painstakingly laid out. In particular, the series of reports he had issued while serving as President Washington's secretary of the treasury represented the clearest summary of his economic and political views. In issuing these reports, Hamilton was not conducting an academic exercise; in his official capacity he was trying to establish the blueprint for the American economy. So it must have been infuriating to see, within just a matter of a few years of his issuing these comprehensive reports, a new president forthrightly declaring a different direction. And not just any president, but his fiercest political rival.

When Jefferson announced that "the sum of good government" was to leave men "free to regulate their own pursuits," he was indeed turning away from Hamilton's grand plan for a government-directed economy. As Hamilton had made clear in his various reports, he did not believe that Americans could or should be left to their own pursuits without government regulation, which is to say, without *his* regulation. He was quite totalitarian-minded on this question. William Graham Sumner remarked in his biography of Hamilton: "He naturally could not consent to a policy which would have dictated to him to hold his rash hands, when his whole being was in a quiver to seize that which he thought was going wrong, and impress upon it at once, and with unshrinking reliance on his own judgment, the form and tendency which he thought best."[2]

Hamilton and Jefferson could not have had more diametrically opposed views on the role of government in the economy. Hamilton was a precursor to the meddling interventionists of the late nineteenth and twentieth centuries, whereas Jefferson had become convinced of the laissez-faire school of economics as espoused by Adam Smith and other writers of that era, especially French economists like Jean-Baptiste Say.

IGNORING ADAM SMITH

If Hamilton was familiar with Adam Smith's great 1776 treatise, *An Inquiry into the Nature and Causes of the Wealth of Nations,* he seems to have had only a superficial (if not incorrect) understanding of much of it. Smith devoted hundreds of pages to explaining why so many of the goods and services sold in the marketplace materialized without anyone—especially anyone in a governmental capacity—being "in charge." His lengthy treatise concluded that individuals, pursuing their own self-interests and fed by a desire to improve their own lives and the lives of their families, will naturally cooperate with others to assure themselves that they will have bread and meat. They don't necessarily have to *care* for one another; they have only to care for themselves and their families. That, it seemed to Smith, was sufficient incentive to create the spark of entrepreneurship that made economic life possible. It was the very key to economic prosperity or "the wealth of nations."

This was Smith's "system of natural liberty." His analysis was not simply a theory he developed in his study; it was based on case studies and historical analysis. *The Wealth of Nations* contained detailed case studies of the division of labor and specialization in woolen coat and pin factories in England, for example. He showed how human cooperation and specialization—laissez-faire capitalism—had led to a thousandfold increase in production using basically the same amount of labor, but just using it smarter. The system Smith identified was one that Jefferson and his followers were well aware of and embraced, as seen in his first inaugural address. Such a system had led to a standard of living that, just a generation or two earlier, would have seemed unimaginable.

In Smith's analysis, government was not to be involved with "planning" any part of the economy; it would provide only for law and order, protection of property and person, national defense, and a basically stable society. Government had a role, in other words, but a very limited and specific one. Smith understood that politicians were every bit as self-interested as anyone else, and that the pursuit of *political* self-interest was almost always at odds with the interests of the masses. When government did become actively involved in economic planning, its laws and regulations would inevitably stifle competition by granting monopoly rights to certain industries, prohibiting foreign competition, and other means. This corrupt scheme, known as mercantilism, tended to benefit politically connected businesses (certainly not all businesses) at the expense of consumers especially and of society as a whole.

Mercantilism was the very model that Hamilton chose to follow when laying out his plans for the American economy. He advocated economic interventionism as a form of economic policy and most clearly articulated his positions in his *Report on Manufactures,* which he delivered to Congress in late 1791. This was the fourth major report Hamilton wrote, after his papers on the public debt and banking. In this report Hamilton showed that he not only dissented from the idea of "natural liberty" in a market economy but also harbored a naive view of politics. He seemed to assume that the policies he advocated would be carried out by

James Madison's "angels" who would act only "for the public good."

Adam Smith observed that manufacturing in England and elsewhere in Europe had developed without any government planning, as though it were led by an "invisible hand." And when government did intervene, it invariably stifled rather than supported industrialization. Hamilton apparently did not believe that such a thing was possible in America. In the *Report on Manufactures* he argued, for example, that most men were such creatures of habit that "the simplest and most obvious improvements" in industry were only adopted "with hesitation, reluctance, and by slow gradations."[3] Even if this were true as a general principle, it is not necessarily a bad thing. It can be argued that "hesitation" and "reluctance" are synonyms for careful business planning, something unknown in government.

Moreover, Hamilton maintained that government intervention in the form of tax-financed subsidies for business was necessary for manufacturing to develop. This is where his theorizing becomes extremely dubious. Government bureaucrats have no way of knowing which industries will thrive and which will not. And because they have no personal financial stake in their decisions, they are *more* prone to making mistakes than would be genuine businessmen.

With private investment, good business decisions (to produce goods or services that please customers) are rewarded with profits; poor business decisions are penalized with losses or bankruptcy. No such market feedback mechanism exists when the government subsidizes business, as Adam Smith and other contemporaries of Hamilton's explained. In fact, government subsidies prop up business failures, sometimes keeping them in existence for years, or decades, at taxpayers' expense. And perversely, the government bureaucrats who dispense the subsidies are not penalized for poor decisions but are often rewarded with bigger budgets, since governments cover up bad decisions by spending even more taxpayer dollars on even more dubious projects. Hamilton the consummate government bureaucrat and political theorist must have been aware of these tendencies. His political opponents certainly were.

In his *Report on Manufactures* Hamilton argued for using the government to try to make certain manufacturing industries appear earlier than they otherwise would on the free market.[4] But this kind of policy would actually *reduce* the wealth of a nation. Industries become economical whenever the benefits of creating the industry outweigh the costs, allowing for profit. If the costs of producing a product are, say, ten times the value of what consumers will pay for it, then resources will be wasted on manufacturing goods that consumers value much less than the resources it takes to produce the goods. This is how the Communist countries of the twentieth century "ate up their capital" and finally collapsed: year after year of using, say, a million dollars' worth of resources to produce products that were worth less than a thousand dollars. Government subsidies only disguise such inefficiencies.

Hamilton also advocated government subsidies for businesses because he thought the fear of failure would deter business formation. In criticizing the Smithian notion that "industry, if left to itself, will naturally find its way to the most useful and profitable employment," Hamilton claimed that there were several reasons for doubting this assertion, including "fear of want of success in untried enterprises" and fear of competing with "those who have previously attained to perfection in the business to be attempted."[5] But again, fear of business failure is not necessarily a bad thing if such fear is based on knowledge that one's product is of marginal (or no) use to consumers. And surely Hamilton must have been aware of the fact that many businesses had successfully competed against rivals who had "attained to perfection" in their respective industries. Competition is a never-ending process, whereby today's "perfectionist" is dethroned (in terms of market share) by tomorrow's newcomer with a better idea. This is how Adam Smith portrayed competition: as a dynamic, rivalrous process of entrepreneurship, a constant struggle to profit by improving one's product and/or reducing its price.

Besides, business development had been occurring for hundreds of years largely without benefit of subsidies. As Nathan Rosenberg and L. E. Birdzell Jr. wrote in *How the West Grew Rich*, "By 1750, three hundred years of gradual expansion in markets had been accompanied by a corresponding expansion in production, both in agriculture and handicrafts."[6] Development was, in fact, occurring all around Hamilton. By the eve of the Revolution New England had already created a highly successful commercial fishing industry that accounted for 10 percent of all exports to Europe. New Englanders pioneered the whale oil industry (the chief source of light at the time) and had become master shipbuilders, with the third-largest maritime fleet in the world.[7] The South and the Mid-Atlantic were primarily agricultural regions, but business entrepreneurship was just as vital there. Farmers had to learn to be businessmen if they were to succeed, especially in extremely competitive foreign markets. By 1776 the American economy was about ten times larger than it had been at the turn of the century.[8]

Hamilton simply discounted all the evidence of how the marketplace functioned as he made his elaborate case for government intervention.

PROTECTIONISM

Much of the system Hamilton laid out in his reports revolved around government protectionism. He was eager to protect "infant" industries, for example. In his *Report on Manufactures* he asserted: "To maintain between the recent establishments of one country and the long matured establishment of another country, a competition upon equal terms, both as to quality and price, is in most cases impracticable. The disparity, in the one or in the other, or in both, must necessarily be so considerable as to forbid a successful rivalship, without the extraordinary aid and protection of government."[9]

But entrepreneurs had over the years revolutionized myriad industries despite the powerful positions of the incumbent businesses in those industries. Again, the spur of competition had proven itself more effective than government subsidies. Consumers are whimsical. Show them a marginally better and/or cheaper version of a product, and they'll drop the old one like it's poison, leaving the "dominant firm" in a position to either improve its performance or go out of business. As the economist Ludwig von Mises wrote: "The consumers . . . make poor people rich and rich people poor. They determine precisely what should be produced, in what quality, and in what quantities. They are merciless egoistic bosses, full of whims and fancies, changeable and unpredictable. . . . They do not care a whit for past merit and vested interests."[10] Nevertheless Hamilton seemed to have little faith in the competitive marketplace without his all-knowing, not-so-invisible, guiding hand.

A major problem with government-subsidized "infant industries" is that they tend to never grow up. The American steel industry, for example, has from its very inception been subsidized in various ways or "protected" from foreign competition with tariffs or quotas on imports. One of the first things President George W. Bush did after his inauguration in 2001 was to impose 50 percent tariffs on foreign steel. The steel industry had *still* not grown up despite 150 years of trade policy "protection." All such "protections" are merely a means of transferring income from consumers to businesses, with the added effect of making the businesses sloppier, *less* efficient, and *less* competitive in world markets.

Hamilton was probably the first to point to the fact that other governments gave away tax dollars to businesses and instituted protective tariffs and quotas to argue that the U.S. government should as well. "[T]he greatest obstacle of all to the successful prosecution of a new branch of industry in a country," Hamilton theorized, "consists . . . in the bounties premiums and other aids which are granted . . . by the nations, in which the establishments to be imitated are previously introduced."[11] Moreover Hamilton contended that "it is evident that the interference and aid" of the U.S. government would be "indispensable" to competing internationally.[12]

This amounts to saying that because other governments embrace corrupt and debilitating economic policies, so should America. In the British mercantilist system, for instance, the government granted monopolies to certain industries. Yes, monopolies in a particular export business would indeed be more profitable than if there were competition. But the profit comes at the expense of the consuming public, which pays higher prices, and of potential competitors. The lack of competition also reduces or eliminates incentives for innovation, cost cutting, and other business improvements. So who benefits from such monopolies? In Britain, it was the king, who granted the monopolies. He effectively became a business partner of the favored monopolists and shared in a larger amount of loot. Hamilton wanted to Americanize this system of crony capitalism. (And his political heirs eventually did, as we will see.)

Hamilton based his protectionism on a number of rather absurd superstitions about international trade. He insisted, for example, that trade barriers that diminished competition would cause *lower* prices. This would suggest that competition causes higher prices and monopoly causes lower prices. Or that politically connected businesses lobby government for protectionist trade policies because they hope the policies will force them to *lower* their prices and make *less* profit. His basic argument was that "internal competition" would somehow become more vigorous if it were isolated from foreign competition, contrary to all worldly experience during his time and ours. And he criticized Adam Smith and others for being too theoretical and not well grounded enough in real-world experience, as he was, supposedly. After summarizing some of Smith's arguments, for example, Hamilton declared that "most general theories, however, admit of numerous exceptions," and he accused Smith's theories of "blending" a "considerable portion of error, with the truths they inculcate."[13] But as noted, Adam Smith did not merely theorize; his work included careful case studies of various British industries and how they had developed over time.

Another superstition Hamilton enunciated was that "transportation is an evil which ought to be minimized, as if it involved pure waste."[14] This was a way of saying that goods imported from Europe, Canada, or elsewhere should be limited or prohibited altogether in order to avoid the "waste" of transportation costs. But at the same time Hamilton supported *interstate* competition, which also involved "evil" transportation costs. Indeed, the Commerce Clause of the U.S. Constitution was invoked to prohibit interstate tariffs and encourage free trade between the states, transportation costs and all.

Transportation costs are the costs of providing a service to consumers. If a man in New York can manufacture a pair of shoes for half of what it costs another shoe manufacturer in Indiana, and he adds another 10 percent to his price for shipping costs, he is still offering a good deal to Indiana customers. On top of that, he will force the less efficient Indiana shoe manufacturer to improve his operations and reduce his costs and prices, further benefiting consumers. (The alternative is that the Indiana manufacturer goes out of business.) Transportation of goods is not a "waste" but an indispensable element of competition.

Ignoring such realities, Hamilton championed protectionist tariffs on imported goods. In the *Report on Manufactures* he claimed that tariffs would enable American manufacturers to "undersell all their foreign Competitors."[15] Well, not necessarily: faced with tariffs on their imports, foreign companies have often responded by cutting their costs and prices to remain competitive in the American market.

In endorsing the protectionist tariff, Hamilton also failed to acknowledge that even if American manufacturers did underprice their foreign competitors, they would still be able to charge higher, *monopolistic prices to consumers* than they would be if there were more competition. They wouldn't face the competitive pressures that drive efficiency and cost cutting. Consumers wouldn't be the only ones to suffer, either. Tariffs on a product like steel that is used to manufacture other goods would place all steel-using manufacturers in America at a competitive *disadvantage* by raising the price of steel. Nor did Hamilton recognize (or at least admit) that tariffs and other forms of protection invite retaliation by America's trading partners, who impose heavy tariffs on American goods that are imported into their countries. He complained quite bitterly about how other governments subsidized some of their own industries with protectionist tariffs, but the possibility of igniting a destructive tariff war doesn't seem to have concerned him.

Hamilton in his report cheerfully claimed that an added benefit of import tariffs would be that they have "the additional recommendation of being a resource of revenue."[16] This claim ignored a basic economic fact of life that Adam Smith and many others were aware of: taxes on imports (tariffs) eventually turn into implicit taxes on exports. That is, tariffs leave America's trading partners with less money with which to purchase American exports.

Another "efficacious means of encouraging national manufactures," wrote Hamilton, would be a complete prohibition of imports altogether, creating "a monopoly of the domestic market."[17] This was one of the oldest mercantilist superstitions—that a nation could increase its wealth by isolating itself economically from the rest of the world and subjecting its citizens to pervasive monopoly. History had long proven such economic isolationism to be a benefit only to governments and their favored monopolists; it impoverished the rest of society by denying it the advantages of the international division of labor. Perhaps the most extreme example of this phenomenon was how China was once one of the most advanced nations in the world—until its government, hundreds of years ago, decided to isolate itself from the rest of the world to supposedly monopolize all of its great inventions and human advances. The result was a decline in Chinese civilization for generations.

Or, looked at in another way, a complete prohibition of imports is what nations at war attempt to do to each other—to strangle the enemy's economy with trade embargoes enforced by naval forces. Hamilton's (and all other protectionists') suggestion to prohibit imports is essentially a suggestion that Americans do to themselves in peacetime what their enemies hope to do to them during wartime.

Yet another naive proposal of Hamilton's was to prohibit "the exportation of the materials of manufactures" so as to impede the progress of foreign competitors.[18] But this would only deprive American exporters of a market for their goods, allowing other foreign suppliers of the same goods to profit instead. If there is a world market for steel, a law that prohibited American steelmakers from supplying steel to Europeans would only create profit opportunities for German and Russian steel manufacturers while doing absolutely nothing to improve American manufacturing.

HAMILTONIAN CORPORATE WELFARE

In addition to calling for subsidies and tariffs, the hyperactive interventionist treasury secretary championed "pecuniary bounties."

Today we would call this "corporate welfare"—giving away tax-payers' funds to businesses. This, he said, would be "one of the most efficacious means of encouraging manufactures"; he added that "in some views" it was "the best."[19]

Hamilton went so far as to argue that for most manufacturing, "bounties" were necessary or "indispensable to the introduction of a new branch" of manufacturing.[20] In a dramatic understatement, he admitted that there was a "degree of prejudice against bounties from an appearance of giving away the public money . . . from a supposition that they serve to enrich particular classes, at the expense of the Community."[21] It is easy to understand why such an "appearance" existed: it was true.

He also acknowledged that there were constitutional questions; Jefferson and Madison, among others, had argued that the Constitution did not allow for such government expenditures. But aha! Hamilton said; the General Welfare Clause could be invoked in defense of bounties. A politician simply needed to argue that bounties were really in the interests of "the general public" and not primarily of the businessmen getting taxpayer money. America's corporate welfare lobbyists have been making that argument ever since.

Together with "pecuniary bounties," Hamilton advocated "premiums." These would be special tax-financed subsidies for "excellence" or "superiority" in manufacturing. Politicians would determine who received the premiums. But, of course, all government spending is determined primarily by politics, not by objective criteria of efficiency, "excellence," or "the public good." As history has shown, such schemes are merely sources of pork-barrel spending, as they allow politicians to effectively buy political support with taxpayer dollars. Hamilton surely must have understood this, for this racket had played out for generations in the European empires he so admired. "Much has been done by this means in Great Britain," he wrote in his *Report on Manufactures*.[22]

The economic foolishness of such an idea lies in the fact that in a market economy the only legitimate judges of excellence are consumers, not politicians. If consumers decide that a product is of excellent quality and competitive price, then the producers of that product will be rewarded with the prize of higher profits. Allowing politicians to dish out subsidies based on *their* perceptions of excellence would only hamper the market economy's operation by diverting resources to businesses that were politically connected but not necessarily very good at serving consumers.

Although Hamilton condemned transportation costs as evil when borne by foreign manufacturers seeking to cater to American consumers, he also proposed the use of tax dollars to *facilitate* the transportation of goods. He argued in his *Report* that private capital markets would not be sufficient to finance the building of roads and canals, so government subsidies would be necessary. He was quickly proven wrong, once again. As the economist Daniel Klein has shown, by 1800—nine years after the publication of the *Report on Manufactures*—some *sixty-nine* private road-building companies had been chartered by the states, and they built new roads "at rates previously unheard of in America."[23] By 1845 more than four hundred roads had been built using private funds. Local merchants invested in the companies because they understood it was clearly in their interest to do so. Entire communities invested, as neighbors persuaded neighbors that it was in the interest of all. Businessmen from larger cities invested in smaller communities because they wanted to expand their markets there.

No governmental coercion was necessary, only persuasion. At least one state—Connecticut—exempted road-building companies from state taxation. The government did not condemn the land needed for roads; rather the road-building companies paid for it in cash and shares of stock.[24] The American spirit of volunteerism prevailed. This was something that Tocqueville would notice immediately but that Hamilton apparently had little or no faith in. Private financing of road (and canal) building may work in "some countries," he wrote, but in a country "like the United States, the public purse must supply the deficiency of private resource."[25] He did not explain why America was unique in this regard among all the nations of the earth.

A number of American states did take Hamilton's advice and used tax dollars to subsidize canal building in early America, but it was generally one big financial disaster in state after state. Perhaps the most spectacular failure occurred in Illinois in the late 1830s. As described by Abraham Lincoln's law partner William Herndon, in 1837 the Illinois legislature, led by Lincoln himself, devoted more than $10 million so that "every river and stream . . . was to be widened, deepened, and made navigable." By these means Illinois would supposedly become "the Empire State of the Union."[26] The whole project turned out to be "reckless and unwise," with the tax burden imposed on the people of Illinois characterized as "monumental in size."[27] None of the grandiose-sounding canal projects was finished. Such debacles were so commonplace that in his history of America, John Bach McMaster concluded that by the 1830s "in every state which had gone recklessly into internal improvements [i.e., government-subsidized road and canal building] the financial situation was alarming. No works were finished; little or no income was derived from them; interest on the bonds increased day by day and no means of paying it save by taxation remained."[28]

TEMPORARY SETBACKS

Alexander Hamilton was so eager to centrally plan the entire economy that in his *Report on Manufactures* he got extremely detailed with his proposals, offering specific examples of how to subsidize many different industries, including iron, copper, lead, coal, wood, skins, grain, flax and hemp, cotton, wool, silk, glass, gunpowder, paper, and books. In this regard he was the prototypical government bureaucrat: he felt he had all the answers.

He did not, of course. Actually, he had a very limited understanding of many areas of economics. William Graham Sumner was right when he characterized Hamilton's *Report on Manufactures* as marred by "confusion and contradiction."[29] Jefferson, for his part, believed that Hamilton larded his reports with high-sounding rhetoric to intentionally befuddle and confuse the average reader. Jefferson believed that Hamilton "was not only a monarchist, but for a monarchy bottomed on corruption" (i.e., mercantilism).[30] Moreover, he interpreted Hamilton's "schemes," as he called them, for public debt, central banking, and subsidies to businesses as "the means by which the corrupt British system of government could be introduced into the United States."[31] He viewed his arguments more as propaganda for the British system than as serious economic analysis. He even wrote to George Washington that Hamilton's ideas "flowed from principles adverse to liberty" and, if enacted, would subvert "step by step the principles of the constitution."[32]

Despite Hamilton's ambitions to remake the American economy according to the proposals he laid out in the *Report on Manufactures*, little came of the report initially. When his rival Jefferson became president, it was a clear blow to his efforts to centrally plan the economy. And just three years after Jefferson's inauguration, Hamilton was dead.

But his economic framework did not die with him. Hamilton's political heirs would embrace his mercantilist model in the years after his death. In fact, in the decades ahead politicians would arm themselves with Hamilton's *Report on Manufactures*, using it as a seemingly authoritative case for government planning of the economy. As William Graham Sumner wrote, the *Report* "proved a welcome arsenal to the politicians" after the War of 1812.[33] An "arsenal" for the accumulation of political power, that is, not for economic development.

THE FORTY-YEAR CAMPAIGN
FOR CRONY CAPITALISM

From the aftermath of the War of 1812 to the early 1860s, the big topics of political debate in the United States were the propriety of protectionist tariffs, "internal improvements subsidies," and a national bank. Henry Clay, leader of the Whig Party and the political inspiration of Abraham Lincoln, would adopt Hamilton's agenda as his own under the rubric of "The American System," a slogan that Hamilton himself coined. As the historian Maurice Baxter writes in *Henry Clay and the American System*, "Clay did not invent [the phrase], for Hamilton had used it more than a quarter century earlier."[34] It was Clay, however, who championed the "system" for a quarter of a century in the U.S. Congress.

Clay picked up the Hamiltonian mantle shortly after Hamilton's death. Beginning his political career as a member of the Kentucky House of Representatives, he ascended to the national stage in 1807 when he stepped in to complete the term of a senator who had resigned.[35] A member of the Kentucky bar, Clay had married the daughter of a wealthy capitalist, and within a few years he had become a powerful landowner and slaveholder.[36] Because of his large hemp crop he became known as "the prince of hemp." He spent decades, literally, advocating protectionist tariffs on foreign hemp; government-subsidized roads and canals, so that he could transport his hemp eastward; and a nationalized bank that could inflate the economy. Not surprisingly, then, he revived Alexander Hamilton's economic agenda—the protectionist tariffs, corporate welfare, and nationalized banking that made up the "American System." (Never mind that this system was not American at all but a rehash of British mercantilism. As Baxter stated, "Clay thought the United States could adopt the British model of industrialization."[37])

Throughout his long political career Clay would repeat Hamilton's dubious arguments for protectionism and corporate welfare. He urged Americans to isolate themselves from world markets and to pursue "economic self sufficiency." He referred to this as the "home market idea" and associated it with "national economic independence" or nondependence on foreign trade.[38] "Let us counteract the policy of foreigners, and withdraw the support we now give to their industry [by purchasing imports], and stimulate that of our own country," he said during an 1824 tariff debate in Congress.[39]

This policy would have crippled the American economy by depriving it of the advantages of the international division of labor, but it would have benefited the hemp producers of Kentucky by banning all foreign hemp. As early as 1810 Clay favored an average tariff rate of 50 percent. He did not get his way then, but tariff rates were increased during the War of 1812 and several times thereafter. On virtually every other issue, too, Clay was busy "confirming a Hamiltonian creed of expansive nationalism," Maurice Baxter wrote.[40]

Most historians are not educated in the field of economics, and political biographers in particular tend to interpret a politician's actions in terms of his *stated* motives. Thus, Baxter makes such statements as "The American system rested on the idea of harmonizing all segments of the economy for their mutual benefit and of doing so by active support from an intervening national government."[41] In reality, the last word one should think of in regard to any kind of central economic planning scheme is *harmony*. The political allocation of resources inevitably creates *conflict*, sometimes armed conflict, as different political factions compete for the "right" to use the coercive powers of the state to benefit themselves economically at the expense of others.

Case in point: Henry Clay and the Whig Party, armed with their Hamiltonian, mercantilist agenda, inflamed political passions and caused sectional strife for decades leading up to the War between the States. For the most part, the protectionist tariffs they proposed benefited manufacturers, and there was relatively little manufacturing in the southern states, even by the 1860s. So tariffs overwhelmingly favored northern states. (Even if some farmers, like hemp farmers from Kentucky, may have benefited.) To southerners, tariffs were all cost and no benefit: they paid higher prices for most of the manufactured goods they bought, from shoes to woolen blankets to farm tools, but were largely unable to pass on their higher cost of living to their customers by raising *their* prices because they sold much of their agricultural produce on very competitive foreign markets. Worse, American protectionist tariffs cut off a large enough amount of foreign trade altogether, since they made America's trading partners poorer.

Consequently, beginning in the early 1820s, there was a sharp regional difference in support for the protectionist element of the Hamilton/Clay "American System." Most northerners supported it, while most southerners opposed it, even though there were some northern free traders (especially in New York City) and some southern protectionists (like the Kentuckian Henry Clay).

In 1824 Clay sponsored a tariff bill that succeeded in doubling the average tariff rate in the United States. Of the 107 votes on the Clay tariff bill in the U.S. House of Representatives, only three votes came from southern states. In the U.S. Senate a mere two out of twenty-five yes votes came from southern states. In 1825 the South Carolina legislature issued a declaration denouncing the entire Hamilton/Clay "American System" of protectionist tariffs, corporate welfare, and nationalized banking system. The legislature characterized Clay's tariff as "a system of robbery and plunder" that "made one section tributary to another."[42]

Nevertheless Clay was emboldened by his success in 1824, and he convinced Congress to increase tariffs even further in 1828, to an average of about 50 percent. Southern politicians immediately condemned the new tariff as the "Tariff of

Abominations." It nearly created a secession crisis some three decades before the War between the States. Virginia, North Carolina, and Alabama joined South Carolina in condemning the 1828 tariff, while legislatures in Massachusetts, Ohio, Pennsylvania, Rhode Island, Indiana, and New York issued resolutions supporting it. The economic and political battle lines were clearly drawn.

South Carolina went so far as to adopt an Ordinance of Nullification in 1832, declaring the "Tariff of Abominations" unconstitutional. The state halted enforcement of the tariff in Charleston harbor, tried to retrieve money that federal tax collectors had already claimed, subjected tariff collectors to fines and imprisonment, and allocated $200,000 to the governor for the purpose of purchasing firearms for the state militia should President Andrew Jackson get serious about collecting the tariff.[43] This hardly sounds like the economic harmony that Maurice Baxter claimed was the nature of the "American System." It was just the opposite: extreme conflict that almost ended up in war.

In contrast to the grandiose motives that Baxter ascribed to Clay, the author Edgar Lee Masters, a well-known playwright and onetime law partner of Clarence Darrow, portrayed him much more accurately:

> Clay was the champion of that political system which doles favors to the strong in order to win and to keep their adherence to the government. His system offered shelter to devious schemes and corrupt enterprises. . . . He was the beloved son of Alexander Hamilton with his corrupt funding schemes, his superstitions concerning the advan-

tage of a public debt, and a people taxed to make profits for enterprises that cannot stand alone. . . . The Whigs adopted the tricks of the pickpocket who dresses himself like a farmer in order to move through a rural crowd unidentified while he gathers purses and watches.[44]

Clay and the Whigs were forced to compromise after their plans provoked South Carolina's outraged response. Clay himself led the effort to enact a lower, compromise tariff in 1833. Around the same time President Andrew Jackson defunded the Bank of the United States, another keystone of the Whigs' "American System." These were low points in the Whigs' history and for Henry Clay as keeper of the Hamiltonian flame. But neither he nor his party (nor their successors, the Republican Party) would give up on the American version of British mercantilism. Clay kept pushing, even as president after president vetoed his "internal improvement" bills.

After the 1840 election, when the Whigs controlled both houses of Congress as well as the White House, Clay surely must have thought that the entire "American System" would finally be rubber-stamped. It probably would have been, too, except that the Whig president, William Henry Harrison, died one month after being inaugurated. His successor, John Tyler, turned out to be a states' rights Jeffersonian who opposed the entire Hamiltonian scheme. President Tyler vetoed a Clay-sponsored bill to resurrect the Bank of the United States and opposed his protectionist tariffs and corporate welfare schemes as well. The Whigs exploded in anger, burning Tyler in effigy in front of the White House and kicking him out of their party.[45]

Just as Edgar Lee Masters said, the "American System" was a scheme of statism and mercantilism under which the majority party used its political power to plunder the minority. As such, it could produce only economic conflict, not harmony. Ultimately, Alexander Hamilton's scheme would be a major cause of civil war.

CHAPTER 6

∽

Hamiltonian Hegemony

[T]he Thirty-seventh Congress [1861–63] ushered
in four decades of neo-Hamiltonianism: government
for the benefit of the privileged few.
—LEONARD P. CURRY, *BLUEPRINT FOR*
MODERN AMERICA: NONMILITARY LEGISLATION
OF THE FIRST CIVIL WAR CONGRESS

The great debate between Jefferson and Hamilton raged on even after those two political rivals passed from the scene. In fact, the contest between their political philosophies would shape American politics for the next half century (and beyond).

Hamilton's successors among the Federalists and later the Whigs would continue the crusade for a centralized government. They understood, as Hamilton had, that only through such monopolistic power over the citizens of the states could the federal government install a mercantilist system—nationalized banking, protectionist trade policy, and corporate welfare.

So the first half of the nineteenth century witnessed Hamiltonians pushing for their twin ambitions of centralized government power and mercantilism. John Marshall and other Federalist judges effectively tried to overturn election results; Henry Clay worked frenetically to impose the Hamiltonian "American System" on the nation; and Federalists and Whigs spread the nationalist mythology about the American founding that Hamilton had begun when he falsely claimed that the states had never been sovereign and that the central government was (and should be) "supreme." Justice Joseph Story, who sat on the U.S. Supreme Court from 1811 to 1845, was "the most Hamiltonian of judges," writes Clinton Rossiter.[1] In his *Commentaries on the Constitution* (1833) Story instructed the legal community and the political elite of the North (mostly) in the Hamiltonian superstition that the union of the "whole people" had somehow created the Constitution, and that the states had played no significant role—an outright falsehood.[2]

Despite all the Hamiltonians' efforts, the Jeffersonians more or less prevailed for decades. The government remained relatively small and decentralized. By the mid-1850s tariff rates were as low as they would be for the entire nineteenth century, and federal subsidies for "internal improvements" were all but nonexistent. The Bank of the United States was dismantled in the 1830s. The American banking system was dominated by state-chartered banks that issued currency backed by gold and silver on demand and that therefore did not inflate their currency beyond what their specie reserves justified. It was not a perfect system, of course, but two highly reputable economic historians, Jeffrey Hummel and Richard Timberlake, have made compelling cases that it was the most stable banking system the United States has *ever* had.[3]

In short, the Hamiltonian economic agenda had been resoundingly defeated time and again. The Hamiltonians had failed to persuade many of their fellow citizens of the alleged virtues of big, centralized government that would primarily benefit the wealthy and politically connected. There was a good deal of support for this agenda in New England and parts of New York, but it was viewed with great suspicion in most other regions of the country.

This all changed in the first years of the War between the States. The Republican Party, which now controlled the government, had inherited the Hamiltonian agenda from the Whigs. No one was more committed to the Hamiltonian cause than President Abraham Lincoln, whom the historian John Lamberton Harper rightly calls "the greatest of [Hamilton's] disciples."[4] Even as a war was being fought and President Lincoln was warning of nothing less than the death of the nation (and indeed of democracy in the world) if the Confederate Army prevailed, the Republicans made it a priority to install Hamiltonian mercantilism, complete with massive taxpayer subsidies to railroad corporations, protectionist tariffs in the range of 50 percent, and a nationalized banking system. And now that Southern Democrats had left the Congress, there was little opposition to their schemes.

As Leonard Curry wrote in *Blueprint for Modern America,* "[C]onstitutional scruples ranked high among the considerations that had prevented Congress from passing a Pacific railway act before 1861." But after southern secession, "constitutional scruples rapidly disintegrated."[5] This is another way of saying that Jefferson's strict constructionism was abandoned in favor of Hamilton's "implied" and "resulting" powers theory of the Constitution, paving the way, at long last, for the triumph of mercantilism in America.

It had been sixty years since the Party of Hamilton enjoyed such political hegemony. But now the neo-Hamiltonians of the Republican Party would monopolize national politics in America, with a few brief exceptions, until Woodrow Wilson's election in 1912.

ALL ABOUT THE MONEY

Abraham Lincoln always declared himself to be "an old Henry Clay Whig." Nearly every member of his cabinet was a former Whig as well and had lobbied for Hamiltonian mercantilism in the form of Clay's vaunted "American System." So it is little surprise that the Lincoln administration moved swiftly to institute the Hamiltonian reforms that its predecessors had failed to enact.

A nationalized banking system was one key element of Alexander Hamilton's agenda that the Lincoln regime resurrected. It did not seem to matter that such a system had been tried twice, with the First and Second Banks of the United States, and each time had created economic instability and corruption. Nor did it matter that during what economists call the "free banking era," which began when the Second Bank of the United States was dissolved in the 1830s, the purchasing power of American currency remained stable. This stability resulted precisely *because* the money supply was denationalized. State governments took a more or less laissez-faire attitude toward banking; about half did not even require a state government charter for individuals who wanted to start a bank, accept deposits, and issue banknotes. Banks, then, were "regulated" mainly by competition in the marketplace: a bank that printed too much currency and did not hold sufficient specie reserves would eventually fail. Such failures did occur, but they remained localized and never caused a national bank panic or depression, as has been the case with nationalized banking systems.

Panics and depressions are what economists refer to as "contagion effects" of centralized or nationalized banking.

There were problems, as there are with any banking system. So-called wildcat banks, for example, would redeem their currency in specie only at branch bank locations in the wilderness, where "not even a wildcat would live." But these were rare events, and the problems were greatly exaggerated by Hamiltonian advocates of the nationalization of money.

The era of free banking was abruptly ended when the neo-Hamiltonian Republicans passed three Legal Tender Acts, beginning in February 1862. These acts of legislation permitted the treasury secretary to issue paper currency (greenbacks) that was not immediately redeemable in gold or silver. Then they passed the National Currency Acts of 1863 and 1864, which created a system of *nationally* chartered (and regulated) banks that could issue currency. A punitive 10 percent tax was placed on state-chartered banks in order to drive them into bankruptcy. The neo-Hamiltonians were candid about their intention to create an "unqualified government monopoly," though they rather absurdly claimed that this would allow "all Americans to share in the advantages of the monopoly."[6] In reality, monopoly is bad for consumers, whether it is a monopoly in steel production, computers, petroleum, or currency. There is no such thing as a "good" monopoly from the consumers' perspective.

The New York banker and congressman Elbridge G. Spaulding helped push the Lincoln administration's nationalized banking legislation through Congress. One reason for the nationalization of the money supply was that banks chartered by the states—northern states—could not always be relied upon to supply infinite amounts of currency, as demanded by the Republican Party to finance its war on the South. Spaulding condemned such banks as "unpatriotic" if not treasonous. Naturally, he invoked Hamilton as his "authority for constitutional interpretation," writes the economic historian Heather Cox Richardson.[7]

Other Republicans likewise cited Hamilton's rationales for a government-run monetary monopoly. Senator John Sherman, who would later become chairman of the powerful U.S. Senate Banking Committee, repeated Hamilton's theory of the usefulness of tying the wealthy to the government. "History teaches us that the public faith of a nation alone is not sufficient to maintain a paper currency," he said. "There must be a combination between the interests of private individuals and the Government." Republican banking legislation would supposedly create "a community of interest between the stockholders of banks, the people, and the government," according to Senator Sherman.[8] He was *almost* right about that. The stockholders of banks would certainly benefit from a monetary monopoly enforced by the government, but "the people" would not. Whenever politicians promote any cause in the name of "the people," you can be sure that the people have had little or nothing to do with the cause and will not benefit from it in any significant way.

The Republican newspaper editor Horace Greeley broadcast this Hamiltonian theory to his reading audience. "The purpose of this measure," he wrote about the 1863 National Currency Act, "is to institute such a connection between the public credit and the banking interest as shall, on the one hand, give the President virtual control of all the banks of the country, and, on the other, make every stockholder and banknote holder in the land an underwriter, so to speak, of the Government bonds . . . effectively harmonizing the interests of both Government and the people."[9] No longer would the public rely on competition and self-interest to "regulate" the banking system; a monetary dictatorship, directed from Washington, D.C., would supposedly be in "the public good," to use another of Hamilton's favorite phrases.

The brother of General William Tecumseh Sherman called for a centralized, government-controlled banking system in order to serve "a powerful national government and an internationally dominant American nation."[10] This call for empire was pure Hamiltonianism also; recall that Hamilton himself urged "more energy" in the national government in pursuit of "imperial glory" and national "splendor."[11]

On March 9, 1863, Alexander Hamilton's hometown newspaper, the *New York Times,* rejoiced that the Lincoln regime's nationalized banking policy "crystallized . . . a centralization of power, such as Hamilton might have eulogized as magnificent."[12] Unfortunately, the results were not so magnificent for Americans. The federal government's printing of greenbacks quickly created enormous inflation. Greenbacks depreciated to a value of only 35 cents' worth of gold by July 11, 1864.[13] The prices of goods purchased by northern-state consumers more than doubled between 1860 and 1865. Most citizens blamed "speculators" or "foreigners" and not their own government, as they should have.[14] They apparently fell for all the phony rhetoric about how such a system would serve "the people."

Because of the inflation it had created, the government itself had to pay more for the war. In his classic book *A History of the Greenbacks,* the economist Wesley Clair Mitchell calculated that it cost northern taxpayers $528 million more.[15] Real wages—that is, wages adjusted for the effects of higher consumer prices or inflation—plummeted as well, as Mitchell determined. And the northern economy as a whole suffered from the fact that businesses could not make rational economic calculations with the constant and unpredictable increases in the price of just about everything. Economic chaos in many industries was the result.

Despite all the neo-Hamiltonians' "public interest" rhetoric about the nationalized banking system, their economic system was an abysmal failure. In the early 1990s three distinguished monetary economists evaluated the overall effects of the National Currency Acts from the time they were enacted in the 1860s until the creation of the Federal Reserve System in 1913. They wrote that the system "was characterized by monetary and cyclical instability, four banking panics, frequent stock market crashes, and other financial disturbances."[16]

But even though the nationalized banking system was a spectacular failure from the economic perspective of the general public, from the neo-Hamiltonians' *political* perspective it was a smashing success. Nationalized banking consolidated political power in Washington. Hamiltonian political hegemony was finally achieved with a monopolized banking system.

THE CURSE OF ECONOMIC ISOLATIONISM

Although Henry Clay, "the prince of hemp," spent much of his long career trying to implement protectionism, within a few years of his death America was as close to free trade as it would be during the entire nineteenth century. But that changed as abruptly as banking policy did with the ascendancy of the neo-Hamiltonians during the Lincoln administration.

The war—and the absence of Southern Democrats—

provided the political sons of Alexander Hamilton with enough political cover to adopt their long-sought policy of extreme protectionism. At the outset of the Lincoln administration the protectionist effort was led by iron manufacturers/congressmen Thaddeus Stevens of Pennsylvania and Justin Morrill of Vermont; New York "ironmaster" Erastus Corning; Representative Valentine Horton, "who was financially interested in both coal mining and salt manufacturing"; and Elbridge Spaulding of New York and John Stratton of New Jersey, who "came from important manufacturing states."[17] The strongest opposition in Congress came from Democrat Clement Vallandigham of Ohio, who proposed repealing the Republicans' protectionist tariff altogether. The Republicans would gerrymander Vallandigham out of his congressional seat and then, a year later, deport him under trumped-up charges of treason for speeches opposing the Lincoln administration.[18]

In addition to the war, northern protectionists used hyped-up nationalism and xenophobia as smoke screens for their real agenda of lining their pockets by monopolizing northern industry. Heather Cox Richardson wrote of "the North's growing antipathy toward Britain, France, and Canada," but what she should have written was *the Republican Party's* antipathy toward these countries. Northern farmers who sold vast quantities of agricultural goods to Europe had no special "antipathy" toward these countries; nor did many other citizens of the northern states.

Nevertheless the propaganda campaign was successful. The Republican Party espoused what Richardson called "an increasingly powerful nationalistic belief that America should concentrate on making itself the wealthiest and strongest nation by enacting prohibitive tariffs, encouraging great industrial development, supporting a strong military, and increasing national pride."[19] This was Hamilton's vision in a nutshell. And none of it could be achieved, the Republicans argued, if foreign competition was allowed.

The neo-Hamiltonians of the 1860s wanted tariffs that would prohibit the importation of *anything* that was made in the United States. Lincoln himself publicly espoused this view. In a speech on the tariff issue he said, "I would continue commerce so far as it is employed in bringing us coffee [which is not grown in the United States], and would discontinue it so far as it is employed in bringing us cotton goods."[20]

Republican Party propagandists became "increasingly angry at Canada" for importing goods into the United States, supposedly causing the federal government to lose millions of dollars in tax revenue.[21] According to Richardson, this "growing dislike of foreigners" that was fed to the public "increased support for the 1862 tariff" and presumably for other tariff increases as well.[22]

The average tariff rate was raised from about 15 percent to 37.2 percent in 1862, and then to 47.06 percent in 1864. It remained in that range or higher for the next fifty years.[23] In addition, the "free list"—the list of manufactured items that were not covered by the tariff law—was cut in half. The great historian of American tariff policy, economist Frank Taussig, wrote that the 1864 tariff increase was not designed to finance the war. It was comprised of tariff "duties whose chief effect was to bring money into the pockets of private individuals."[24] He was referring, of course, to northern manufacturers, who would be isolated from foreign competition by the tariffs, thereby allowing them to charge higher prices and earn unprecedented profits. And this was at a time when their government was at war and presumably in need of *less* expensive manufactured goods for the war effort.

With a president who had a long history as a protectionist, a cabinet made up almost entirely of Henry Clay Whigs, and a neo-Hamiltonian Congress, the Republican Party went on a tariff-increasing binge for several decades. Recommendations for 100 percent tariff rates on many items were commonplace, according to Taussig, and "the protective system" included "almost every article, whatever its character, whose production in the country is possible."[25]

The ultimate goal of the neo-Hamiltonian protectionists of the 1860s (and beyond) was what economists call "autarky," or economic isolationism. They wanted to completely isolate America from most foreign trade in order to establish monopolies or oligopolies (competition among the very few) in various industries—industries in which quite a few of the Republican politicians of the day were personally invested. They did not totally succeed, but they did prevail in imposing extremely high tariff rates for half a century after the war.

The major danger of economic isolationism is that a nation divorces itself from the international division of labor. Individuals and businesses all around the world have various specialties, and a business will become stronger and more profitable if it can purchase its supplies from whoever offers it the best deal, whether that partner is from the United States, Canada, or anywhere else. Protectionists know this; that's why they invariably advocate protectionism for the things that they sell but free trade for the things that they buy, such as parts and materials that they use to manufacture their own products.

Another danger that has often been realized is retaliation: foreign governments do not always sit on their hands while the U.S. government harms their economies with protectionism. They retaliate, blocking the importation of American goods into their countries.

Abolishing the international division of labor is a recipe for economic disaster, but that is exactly the economic policy recipe that the nineteenth-century neo-Hamiltonians cooked up for America. It is fortunate that they succeeded only as far as they did and did not realize Lincoln's professed goal of choking off all international competition.

It was the American *consumer* who was most harmed by this protectionism. Prices in "protected" industries were higher, product quality was lower, and innovation was stifled because competitive pressures were weakened.

Other manufacturers were hurt as well. American manufacturers that imported "capital goods"—that is, goods used in the production of other items—were placed at a competitive disadvantage, since the tariffs increased *their* costs of production and made *their* products less competitive in world markets.

American exporters, especially American farmers, were harmed tremendously, because they sold a large share of their product on foreign markets—the very markets that American protectionism was designed to make poorer. Recognizing that prohibitive tariffs would make America's trading partners less capable of purchasing American agricultural products, the neo-Hamiltonians in the Lincoln administration attempted to "buy off" farmers by establishing the U.S. Department of Agriculture, which promised corporate welfare of a sort for *them* too.

It is hard to believe that a man as politically astute as Alexander Hamilton, or any of his political descendants, from Clay to Lincoln, would not have recognized that as soon as protectionism was established, it would create a powerful lobbying force for more and more protectionism—and for making it permanent. As the economist Murray Rothbard once said, "infant industries" that are protected by tariffs not only never grow up, they tend to become "senile industries," relying on protection from competition *forever.* The American steel industry, as we have seen, is a case in point.

The economically uneducated who write about this period, which includes most historians, usually fall into the trap of the "post hoc, ergo propter hoc" fallacy: they assume that since protectionist tariffs existed, and the American economy grew, the tariffs must have *caused* the economic growth. The truth is that the American economy grew in the latter half of the nineteenth century *despite* neo-Hamiltonian protectionism, not because of it. American industry grew rapidly during the late nineteenth century because of entrepreneurial inventiveness, technological change, capital investment, reduced transportation costs, the growth of large corporations and the invention of management methods, the increased sophistication of financial markets, the absence of income taxation, and the expansion of free labor (which is always more productive than slave labor) after the War between the States.[26] All of this was able to overcome the drag on the economy created by the Republican Party's mercantilist tariff policy. Without the tariffs, the American economy would have grown even faster.

America adopted protectionism when much of the rest of the world was embracing free trade. England abolished tariffs in 1850.

The British were bankrupting themselves with the cost of empire, and free trade was their one economic blessing. France and much of the rest of Europe were also moving away from mercantilism, thanks to the efforts of such free-trade crusaders as the French writer Frédéric Bastiat. But thanks to the neo-Hamiltonian Republican Party, protectionism stuck in America.

OPENING THE FLOODGATES
OF CORPORATE WELFARE

Republicans also enacted the third element of Alexander Hamilton's mercantilist agenda: corporate welfare. As of 1861, no federal government program of any significance had subsidized corporations for road, canal, or railroad building. There had been many experiments at the state level, and every one of them was a financial disaster. In the typical scenario, Whig politicians would promise a commercial empire if only the state legislature would earmark millions to build roads, canals, and railroads. When legislatures followed through, little or nothing would actually be built; millions would be stolen; and the states' taxpayers would be left with a public debt that would take decades to pay off. State government experiments with Hamiltonian corporate welfare during the first half of the nineteenth century were so disastrous that by 1875 only one state—Massachusetts—had not *amended its constitution* to prohibit such expenditures of public funds.[27]

But the War between the States once again enabled the Republicans to adopt part of the Hamiltonian scheme that Henry Clay and others had been unable to achieve. In Congress the opposition was again led by Congressman Vallandigham of Ohio, whose party was hopelessly outnumbered. He was one of the few remaining Jeffersonians in a government completely dominated by Hamiltonians.

There was no economic necessity for government subsidies to build a transcontinental railroad, as the railroad entrepreneur James J. Hill would prove by building and profitably running the Great Northern without a penny of subsidy, not even land grants.[28] The lack of economic necessity did not affect the plans of the neo-Hamiltonians, however. The leader of their party, Abraham Lincoln, was a longtime railroad industry lawyer and insider, and the northern railroads, manufacturers, and banks were their main political constituency, just as merchants and bankers were Hamilton's constituency. The railroads had done as much as anyone to elect a Republican president, and they expected to be "rewarded."

As an attorney, Lincoln had represented the Illinois Central, Chicago and Alton, Ohio and Mississippi, Rock Island, and Chicago and Mississippi railroads. He had even been offered the position of chief counsel of the New York Central.[29] He was a consummate railroad industry insider who traveled around the Midwest in a private train car courtesy of the Illinois Central, accompanied by an entourage of company executives. There was never any doubt that at long last, Hamiltonian "bounties" would be paid to the railroad industry.

So in June 1861, just two months after Fort Sumter and with the country at war, Lincoln called a special emergency session of Congress to begin work on the Pacific Railway Act. The legislation was signed into law in 1862. At that point the president had the right to choose the eastern terminus of the transcontinental railroad; he chose Council Bluffs, Iowa—where he had invested in land in 1857.[30]

Many Republican congressmen and supporters became wealthy because of the Pacific Railway Act. Congressman Thaddeus Stevens of Pennsylvania "received a block of [Union Pacific Corporation] stock in exchange for his vote" on the bill, wrote Dee Brown, the historian of the American West.[31] He also demanded, as a condition of his vote, that the law be written so that all iron used to build and equip the railroad be American-manufactured iron. So Stevens the steel manufacturer championed protectionist tariffs on iron and steel, which increased the price of those items. Then he manipulated the new railroad law to guarantee that the government would not be able to economize on behalf of the taxpayers by purchasing lower-priced foreign steel. Similarly, Congressman Oakes Ames of Massachusetts "became a loyal ally" of the railroad legislation, wrote Brown, when he and his brother were promised the manufacturing contract for shovels.[32] It must have taken a lot of shovels to dig railroad beds from Iowa to California.

Once the subsidies started pouring in, the seemingly insatiable railroad corporations lobbied for more and more. They "mushroomed into one of the most powerful and ruthless lobbies that the republic had ever known," wrote the historian Leonard Curry.[33] The two railroad corporations established by the Pacific Railway Act—the Union Pacific and Central Pacific—were paid subsidies by the mile. This gave them an incentive to build quickly and often inefficiently. If the road collapsed after spring rains, it meant even more profits in return for rebuilding the shoddy railroad line.

In addition to this source of inefficiency, many members of

Congress from the western states and territories demanded a line to their district in return for their vote for additional subsidies. Consequently, myriad uneconomical rail lines were built for political reasons. This, and other kinds of regulation-in-return-for-subsidies, only put the railroads in need of more subsidies. All the risks of the enterprise were socialized—paid for by the taxpayers—whereas all of the profits went to private individuals as owners of stock in the companies.

Much of the subsidy to railroad corporations came in the form of land grants—100 million acres' worth. This rendered the Homestead Act a failure, since that act's purpose was to give away free land to homesteaders, not to politically connected corporations.[34] Only about 19 percent of the land went to farmers; the rest was snapped up by wealthy speculators and corporations. As Leonard Curry has written, "In the postwar era, public lands were handed over to private transportation interests, while legislation ostensibly designed to assist the farmers [i.e., the Homestead Act] was notoriously ineffective."[35]

More subsidies arrived in the 1880s, as Congress began appropriating more than $8 million per year for "river and harbor bills." After a seventy-five-year political battle, the federal government had embraced Alexander Hamilton's "internal improvement" spending. Today we know it as "pork barrel spending."[36]

A predictable consequence of Hamiltonian corporate welfare was massive graft and corruption. That soon came in the postwar era in the form of the so-called Crédit Mobilier scandal. Crédit Mobilier was a corporation that the Union Pacific Railroad contracted with to build part of the rail line from Nebraska to California. Among the company's investors were Congressmen Oakes Ames, John B. Alley, and Samuel Hooper, all of Massachusetts, and Senator James W. Grimes of Iowa. These men, and others who assisted them, conspired to have the company bill the government for about twice the actual cost of building the railroad line. The company's management pocketed some $30 million in profits, while those with inside information about this taxpayer swindle were able to purchase shares of stock for $5 per share that soon became worth more than $100.[37]

To keep this scheme secret, Congressman Ames bribed his fellow members of Congress and members of the Grant administration by offering them shares of stock in the Union Pacific and Crédit Mobilier companies. He ended up bribing an honor roll of New England and Upper Midwest Yankees, among them Vice President Schuyler Colfax; Senators Henry Wilson of Massachusetts, James Patterson of New Hampshire, and John Logan of Illinois; Speaker of the House James Blaine of Maine; and Congressmen W. D. Kelley of Pennsylvania, James Garfield of Ohio, James Brooks of New York, John Bingham of Ohio, Henry Dawes of Massachusetts, and Glenni Scofield of Pennsylvania.[38]

The whole sordid mess became public in the summer of 1872 when one of the conspirators, Henry S. McComb of Delaware, became engaged in an intense feud with Oakes Ames and in response published a list of members of Congress whom Ames had bribed.

As notorious as the Crédit Mobilier scandal was, it was only the tip of the iceberg of the kind of corruption and waste of taxpayers' dollars that would be the inevitable—and perfectly predictable—consequence of the "American System" of corporate welfare.

THE TRIUMPH OF HAMILTONIAN "CONSERVATISM"

The American public was outraged by the Crédit Mobilier scandal and by subsequent scandals involving direct government subsidies or "bounties" to business. In response, they demanded more political control of business—not understanding that political control was the *problem,* not the solution. Alexander Hamilton's phony "public interest" theory of government regulation continued to fool Americans and would do so for many decades to come.

In fact, nearly a century later scholars still clung to the theory that increased federal government regulation of business was a response to "market failure." But in the important and influential 1963 book *The Triumph of Conservatism,* the historian Gabriel Kolko meticulously documented how American businesses, far from resisting political control, *sought* such regulation because they could use it to their advantage.[39] "[T]he regulation itself," Kolko wrote, "was invariably controlled by leaders of the regulated industry, and directed toward ends they deemed acceptable or desirable."[40] Some thirty years later the legal scholar Butler Shaffer echoed Kolko's views, writing of an increased recognition among scholars that "government regulation has generally served to further the very economic interests being regulated" and that the advantages businesses sought were those "denied them in the marketplace."[41]

Kolko recognized the origins of this massive regulatory system: he called it "a reincarnation of the Hamiltonian unity of politics and economics" and "the new Hamiltonianism."[42] And it had become yet another curse on the American economy.

The history of these government regulatory schemes showed

that the creation of a monopoly could be just as valuable as, if not more valuable than, a cash grant from the government. Consider the Interstate Commerce Commission (ICC), created in 1887. While the ICC had been established ostensibly to regulate the railroads "in the public interest" (there's Hamilton's favorite phrase again), the railroad industry had in fact lobbied for it. The first head of the ICC was a former railroad company president. One of the first things the commission did was to outlaw customer discounts, such as those that Cornelius Vanderbilt was granting to major customers who transported thousands of barrels of kerosene and other petroleum products by rail. By making discounts illegal, the ICC relieved railroad companies from the pressure to compete for customers.

Similarly, American businesses had pushed the federal government to place strict regulatory standards on imported food and drug products as a form of veiled protectionism. The result was, as Kolko noted, the Food and Drug Administration (FDA). Big businesses also understood that costly federal regulation would disproportionately harm their smaller competitors. Thus while claiming to be "socially responsible" by favoring regulation of their own industries, businesses really supported the creation of monopoly power in their industry, solely to their own economic benefit.

Teddy Roosevelt was a "progressive era" president (and admirer of Hamilton) who is credited with being a great environmentalist for having nationalized thousands of acres of land and built dams and other "conservation" projects with taxpayer dollars. But this, too, was a form of neo-Hamiltonian corporate welfare. Mining, farming, timber, and other interests lobbied for these programs because they would be enriched with "free" dams and irrigation, waterway improvements, cheap, subsidized water (mostly for agriculture), cheap timber lands (leased for next to nothing from the government), and cheap access to grazing lands.

One of the worst examples of "the new Hamiltonianism" in the early twentieth century was the creation of government franchise monopolies in all the utilities industries—natural gas, electricity, telephone service, water supply, and so forth. These industries were all fiercely competitive in the late nineteenth and early twentieth centuries, and that competition was driving down prices, creating incentives for innovation, and encouraging good customer service. As the UCLA economist Harold Demsetz pointed out in a book on the economics of competition:

> Six electric light companies were organized in the one year of 1887 in New York City. Forty-five electric light enterprises had the legal right to operate in Chicago in 1907. Prior to 1895, Duluth, Minnesota, was served by five electric lighting companies, and Scranton, Pennsylvania, had four in 1906. . . . During the latter part of the nineteenth century, competition was the usual situation in the gas industry in this country. Before 1884, six competing companies were operating in New York City. . . . [C]ompetition was common and especially persistent in the telephone industry. . . . Baltimore, Chicago, Cleveland, Columbus, Detroit, Kansas City, Minneapolis, Philadelphia, Pittsburgh, and St. Louis, among the larger cities, had at least two telephone services in 1906.[43]

This was all to the benefit of consumers, but the utility businesses were inconvenienced by having to compete. So a different type of competition began—in the political arena. The utilities began lobbying state and local governments to grant them monopoly franchises. All kinds of theories were invented to rationalize the monopolies. They would supposedly eliminate "wasteful duplication" of facilities, for example, as though it is possible for two manufacturing businesses to compete without "duplicating" their factories. The superstition was also invented that actual competition would somehow lead to monopoly anyway, with one large firm dominating each industry—this despite the fact such "natural monopolies" had never occurred.

All this theorizing apparently provided politicians with enough cover to grant monopolies in all the utility industries to politically connected businesses, in return for financial support, some legal and some not. State and local governments essentially shared in the loot collected by the utility monopolies. In his book *The Gas Light Company of Baltimore,* George T. Brown offered a good example of how utility monopolies were created. In 1890, at a time when there were three competing gas companies in Baltimore, the Maryland legislature introduced a bill calling "for an annual payment to the city from the Consolidated Gas Company of $10,000 a year and 3 percent of all dividends declared in return for the privilege of enjoying a 25-year monopoly."[44] This type of scheme occurred in every state, leading the University of Illinois economist Horace Gray to comment that "the public utility status was to be the haven of refuge for all aspiring monopolists who found it too difficult, too costly, or too precarious to secure and maintain monopoly by private action alone."[45]

The same story can be told of the radio, real estate, milk, airline, coal, oil, and agricultural industries, to name a few. Consider what happened with the telephone industry. By the beginning of the twentieth century, a dozen years after AT&T's initial patents expired, there were more than three thousand telephone companies in America. Some states had as many as two hundred telephone companies operating simultaneously. AT&T started out with a patent monopoly on telephone service, but it had lost more than half of the market to competition, and prices were being driven down sharply by the competition. So after World War I the company created a formidable lobbying force and persuaded every state to grant it another monopoly in telephone service and to make competition illegal—all supposedly "in the public interest."[46]

NEW DEAL HAMILTONIANS

Modern-day Hamiltonians like the writer Michael Lind refer to all of these mercantilist policies as "economic nationalism," a phrase that implies the policies somehow benefit the entire nation. They claim that such policies were finally embraced nationally during FDR's New Deal, and they are right, at least with regard to corporate welfare. The hallmarks of FDR's "First New Deal" (1933–34) were the National Industrial Recovery Act and the Agricultural Adjustment Act. The former law created the National Industrial Recovery Administration (NIRA), which attempted to create a cartel in every manufacturing industry by adopting "price codes"— government-imposed controls that artificially pushed prices up. This system reflected FDR's belief in the convoluted and false theory that low prices had caused the Great Depression.

More than seven hundred industry "price codes" were adopted and enforced by literally thousands of code police, led by a former army general named Hugh Johnson. The code police were so heavy-handed that a lowly New York tailor named Jack Magid was arrested, convicted, fined, and imprisoned for pressing a men's suit for 35 cents when the Tailor's Code set the price at 40 cents.[47] Six thousand statisticians were employed to dream up the "correct" prices for thousands of consumer items. The oil industry was monopolized by a law that restricted the amount of oil that could be sold in interstate and international commerce, thereby pushing up the price of petroleum and petroleum products.

The NIRA was an extreme form of Hamiltonian mercantilism. This country has never seen a closer relationship between business and government. Of course, it all only made the Great Depression worse. Monopolies tend to reduce production in order to charge higher prices. Reduced production is always accompanied by reduced employment. What was needed was *more* production, which would have led to more employment.

The Agricultural Adjustment Administration (AAA) attempted a similar plan with regard to agriculture, using various regulatory means to force or bribe farmers to grow fewer crops and raise less livestock in an attempt to push up the price of food. Poor sharecroppers in the southern states were especially devastated by this program of *reducing* agricultural production (and employment).

John T. Flynn, one of the most prominent critics of FDR, noted the similarity between the First New Deal in America and economic fascism in Italy. Mussolini "organized each trade or industrial group or professional group into a state-supervised trade association. He called it a cooperative. These cooperatives operated under state supervision and could plan production, quality, prices, distribution, labor standards, etc." The NIRA in America "provided that in American industry each industry should be organized into a federally supervised trade association. It was not called a cooperative. It was called a Code Authority. But it was essentially the same thing. . . . [T]his was fascism."[48]

More precisely, it was *economic* fascism without the racism, dictatorship, and other ugly features of European and Japanese fascism. It was indeed almost identical to how the European and Japanese fascists attempted to centrally plan their economies. Hamilton's curse had gone international.

HAMILTON'S ULTIMATE TRIUMPH

Nationalized banking, protectionism, and corporate welfare—all these plans originated with Alexander Hamilton and were ultimately put into effect during the Lincoln administration. While the Republicans might have justified these plans as wartime measures, they lasted for decades after the War between the States ended.

And those three mercantilist schemes were just part of Hamilton's vision for America that came to pass during the Lincoln administration. Perhaps most important of all was the plan Hamilton laid out at the Constitutional Convention for a kinglike "permanent president," by means of which political power would be consolidated in the nation's capital and states' rights would effectively be abolished. Hamilton failed to achieve this objective at the Constitutional Convention, but seventy-five years later his political heirs would fulfill his ambitions.

Generations of historians have labeled Abraham Lincoln a "dictator," although supposedly a benevolent one. "Never had the power of a dictator fallen into safer hands," wrote James Ford Rhodes, author of a multivolume history of the United States.[49] "If Lincoln was a dictator, it must be admitted that he was a benevolent dictator," announced the Lincoln biographer James G. Randall.[50] Many other historians have made similar comments. The "dictator" references are no accident. The plain historical fact is that Lincoln *did* ignore the Constitution and effectively declare himself dictator. He began a war without the consent of Congress; unilaterally and illegally suspended the writ of habeas corpus; imprisoned tens of thousands of northern political dissenters; censored all telegraph communications; confiscated firearms in the border states in violation of the Second Amendment; deported Democratic Congressman Clement Vallandigham for his outspoken anti-administration speeches; issued an arrest warrant for the chief justice of the United States, Roger B. Taney, after he issued an opinion that only Congress and not the president could suspend habeas corpus; illegally orchestrated the secession of West Virginia from Virginia; and shut down several hundred opposition newspapers in the North, in some cases imprisoning the editors and owners. "This amazing disregard for the . . . Constitution was considered by nobody as legal," wrote the historian Clinton Rossiter in his book *Constitutional Dictatorship.*[51]

Although Lincoln did not become a "permanent" president, the precedents he established have endured to this day. Countless American politicians and pundits have cited those precedents to rationalize trampling on the liberties of their fellow citizens and various other unconstitutional governmental actions, especially undeclared wars.[52]

Lincoln also permanently altered the relationship between the federal government and the states, creating the dominant central power that Alexander Hamilton had desired. By 1865 the Jeffersonian tradition of states' rights—by which the citizens were the masters rather than the servants of their government—had been all but eradicated. American citizens no longer possessed the rights of nullification (of unconstitutional federal laws) and secession and thus could no longer serve as a popular check on the powers of the central state. This, of course, was Alexander Hamilton's ultimate end.

But the final blow to federalism, and the final realization of Hamilton's vision, would not come until the fateful year of 1913.

CHAPTER 7

~

The Hamiltonian Revolution

of 1913

The freedoms won by Americans in 1776 were lost in the revolution of 1913.

—FRANK CHODOROV,
THE INCOME TAX: ROOT OF ALL EVIL

Hamiltonian political hegemony, including the near-death of the principle of states' rights or federalism, was achieved during the War between the States. But the citizens of the once-sovereign states still retained *some* control over the government in Washington after the war. The Jeffersonian states' rights tradition, therefore, had some life in it yet.

But that life was snuffed out completely in one revolutionary year, 1913. During that one year three sweeping changes occurred: the Seventeenth Amendment to the Constitution was ratified, and so for the first time U.S. senators would be directly elected rather than appointed to office by state legislatures; the federal income tax was adopted; and the Federal Reserve System was created. All three institutions almost completely centralized power in Washington and constituted the death blow to the old Jeffersonian tradition in American politics—and the final, decisive victory for the Hamiltonians. Hamilton's totally centralized government, with an increasingly arrogant chief executive who could bully and manipulate the governors and legislatures of the states (as well as their citizens), was finally realized 126 years after he first enunciated his plan at the Constitutional Convention. The world would soon discover that national borders would not limit the bullying, interventionist proclivities of American presidents.

THE SEVENTEENTH AMENDMENT

Whenever the topic of federalism comes up today in the media or in academic writings, it is usually discussed in the context of some recent Supreme Court decision relating to the division of political power between the federal government and the states. But that was not what the founders had in mind. They never intended federalism to be enforced or protected by a few government lawyers with lifetime tenure. Indeed, the Jeffersonians believed that such a thing would be a complete farce.

If federalism or states' rights was to be protected, it would be the responsibility of the citizens of the sovereign states, through their elected state representatives. Allowing the federal government to make such decisions would simply be allowing the fox to guard the henhouse. As part of the political infrastructure of federalism, also known as divided sovereignty, the Constitution established that U.S. senators would be appointed by state legislators.

Ralph Rossum of Claremont McKenna College explains the rationale for this in his book *Federalism, the Supreme Court, and the Seventeenth Amendment.* The Constitution's framers intended that state legislatures would appoint senators and then instruct them on how to vote in Congress. This was to safeguard against the corruption of senators by special interests seeking federal legislation that would be good for them but bad for the general public. "The ability of state legislatures to instruct senators was mentioned frequently during the Constitutional Convention and the state ratifying conventions and was always assumed to exist," writes Rossum, but still this notion "went unchallenged."[1]

During the subsequent debates over ratification, the matter of having state legislatures instruct senators came up repeatedly. At the New York ratifying convention, John Jay, who, along with James Madison and Hamilton himself, wrote *The Federalist Papers,* said: "The Senate is to be composed of men appointed by the state legislatures; they will certainly choose those who are most distinguished for their general knowledge. I presume they will also instruct them, that there will be a constant correspondence between the senators and the state executives, who will be able, from time to time, to afford them all that particular information which particular circumstances may require."[2] At the Massachusetts ratifying convention Fisher Ames referred to U.S. senators as "ambassadors of the states."[3]

In *Federalist* no. 45 Madison wrote that since "the Senate will be elected . . . by the State Legislatures," it "will owe its existence more or less to the favor of the State Governments, and must consequently feel a dependence."[4] Because of this, wrote Madison, the U.S. Senate "would be disinclined to invade the rights of the individual States, or the prerogatives of their governments."[5] In *Federalist* no. 62 Madison emphasized that this system recognized and reaffirmed that the states were of course sovereign, as it gave "to state governments such an agency in the formation of the federal government as must secure the authority of the former."[6]

After the Constitution was adopted various statesmen continued to voice their opinions about the importance of senators being appointed and not elected by the populace. Roger Sherman of Connecticut wrote in 1789 that because senators were appointed by the state legislatures they "will be vigilant in supporting their [the states'] rights against infringement by the legislative or executive of the United States."[7] The Virginia Jeffersonian St. George Tucker, who edited *Blackstone's Commentaries* for the American audience, wrote that if a senator "abuses his confidence," he would "be sure to be displaced."[8] Even the prototypical Hamiltonian nationalist, Joseph Story, wrote in his *Commentaries on the Constitution of the United States* that state legislative appointment of senators would avoid "undue encroachments of the powers of the states."[9]

Most of the founders understood that it would never be in the self-interest of the federal judiciary to limit federal power for the benefit of the states. "They clearly did not intend that the undemocratic Supreme Court would protect the original federal design," writes Rossum.[10] For as the Anti-Federalist writer "Brutus" remarked, "every extension of the power of the general legislature, as well as of the judicial powers, will increase the powers of the courts." And along with increased power usually comes increased monetary compensation and perquisites. Americans should never fall for the Hamiltonian notion that the central government can be trusted to act "for the common good," in other words.

The states quickly showed that they would exercise their right to challenge the federal government's decisions by means of their control over senators. The famous Kentucky and Virginia Resolves of 1798, authored by Thomas Jefferson and James Madison, were written in response to the obnoxious Sedition Act passed by Congress and were intended to be used by the Kentucky and Virginia legislatures to instruct their senators to vote to repeal the act.

Especially during the pre-1865 era senators took their instructions from state legislatures very seriously. John Quincy Adams resigned his Senate seat in 1809 because he disagreed with the Massachusetts state legislature's instructions to oppose the Jefferson/Madison trade embargo. Senator David Stone of North Carolina resigned in 1814 after his state legislature disapproved of his collaboration with New England Federalists on several legislative issues. Senator Peleg Sprague of Maine resigned in 1835 after opposing his state legislature's instructions to oppose the rechartering of the Bank of the United States. When the U.S. Senate censured President Andrew Jackson for having vetoed the rechartering of the Bank, several state legislatures instructed their senators to seek to have Jackson's censure expunged. Seven southern senators resigned rather than obey these instructions. One of them was Senator John Tyler of Virginia, who would become president in 1841 after the death of President William Henry Harrison, one month after Harrison was inaugurated.[11]

The support for state legislative appointment of senators was so strong that even nationalists of the founding generation— Hamilton and his allies—paid lip service to the principle. At the Massachusetts ratifying convention Rufus King—who would become Hamilton's political point man in the U.S. Senate—had argued that "the state legislatures, if they find their delegates erring, can and will instruct them."[12] At the Connecticut convention Oliver Wolcott referred to the states as "the pillars which uphold the general system" of the Constitution, "without whose assent no public act can be made," since senators would be "appointed by the states, and will secure the rights of the several states."[13] Hamilton himself had said at the New York ratifying convention that if the people wanted to make a change in their government or its policies, "they have it in their power to instruct their representatives; and the state legislatures, which appoint the senators, may enjoin it also upon them."[14]

But after issuing many such assurances that states' rights would be protected by the Constitution, Hamilton and his Federalist partners would work diligently to destroy those rights. In fact, they and their political heirs waged an almost century-long campaign to abolish this check upon the powers of the central state. It could never have been any other way. The Jeffersonians championed the appointment of senators by state legislators for reasons that were anathema to Hamilton, the Federalists, the Whigs, and the Republicans—namely, it limited the size and scope of the central state. In *Federalist* no. 10 James Madison remarked that the whole purpose of the Constitution was to control "the violence of faction," by which he meant special-interest politics. The appointment of senators by state legislatures was one of the constitutional constructs that was intended to assist in this goal. It did so by limiting senators' ability to sell their votes to special-interest groups nationwide. After all, senators who went to Washington and voted against the interests of their home-state constituents could and would be replaced on short notice by their state legislatures; the founders well understood that it is easier to manipulate the public than to fool professional politicians who follow the issues intently.

"Not surprisingly," Ralph Rossum writes, it was a Federalist from New York, Congressman Henry Randolph Storrs, who introduced the first resolution calling for direct election of senators. Storrs did so on February 14, 1826. "From that date

until the adoption of the Seventeenth Amendment eighty-six
years later," Rossum documents, "187 subsequent resolutions of
a similar nature were also introduced before Congress, 167 of
them after 1880."[15] The flurry of resolutions starting toward the
end of the century was no accident; it coincided with the rise of
the "Progressives."

The so-called Progressives worshipped the god of democracy and therefore championed the direct election of senators by
saying it would make government more "democratic." The founding generation, especially the Jeffersonian wing, had not been so
naive about politics, viewing democracy as at best a necessary evil
that needed to be controlled and limited. But the Progressives
made great gains with the American public by waging a massive
propaganda campaign against the Founding Fathers and their
views of the Constitution.

One of the Progressives' main arguments, oddly, was that the
direct election of senators would *reduce* political corruption. Corruption does infect all levels of politics, but the founding generation—unlike the Progressives—understood that the public was
more likely to detect and limit corruption the closer the government is to the people. Who in America today would believe that
opening the door for senators (or prospective senators) to raise
campaign funds from anywhere, including foreign countries,
would limit rather than invite corruption?

Other rationales for the Seventeenth Amendment were also
dubious. One argument was that states often became deadlocked
in deciding who to appoint as their senators, leading to underrep-
resentation for long periods of time. But the cause of this problem
was the complicated voting rules that the federal government—in
a usurpation of power—had forced on the states in the 1870s. A

simple solution would have been to allow the states to use a simple plurality vote.

In any case, Congress pushed through the Seventeenth Amendment in May 1912. Massachusetts, the home base of the old Federalist coalition, became the first state to ratify the amendment. On April 8, 1913, the direct election of senators was enshrined as the new law of the land after Connecticut became the requisite thirty-sixth state to ratify the amendment.

Rossum argues that most political leaders who supported the Seventeenth Amendment simply did not understand the founders' logic. This is most unlikely; in fact, there is every reason to believe that most of them understood it perfectly well. The issue, rather, was most likely that politicians *rejected* the logic of limited constitutional government because it limited their *own* powers. Armed with charges of state-level corruption, and fanciful theories of democracy put forth by "Progressive" intellectuals, they made their power grab.

It worked. Todd Zywicki of George Mason University Law School has noted that since 1913 we have seen a "ratchet effect," whereby the federal government uses the pretext of war or some other crisis to increase taxes or regulations, commandeer more resources, water down civil liberties, and otherwise expand federal governmental power, but then does not return the government to its original size or mission once the crisis ends.[16] Zywicki explains that this ratchet effect was largely absent prior to 1913 because the citizens of the states were then more capable of controlling their "Leviathan" government.[17] In his words, "[S]tatistical and anecdotal evidence suggests that the Senate played an active role in preserving the sovereignty and independent sphere of action of state governments. Rather than delegating lawmaking authority to Washington, state legislators insisted on keeping authority close to home. . . . As a result, the long-term size of the federal government remained fairly stable and relatively small during the pre-Seventeenth-Amendment era."[18]

Rossum writes, "Since 1913, there has been a profound increase in the number and intrusiveness of congressional measures invading the residuary sovereignty of the states."[19] Those measures began almost immediately, with the federal government infringing upon the police powers of the states to regulate, regiment, and control the economy. To pander to labor union pressure, Congress passed a federal child labor act in 1916. Unions promoted such legislation not because they were necessarily concerned about the well-being of teenagers in the workplace but because young people rarely belonged to unions and were therefore a form of competition to unionized labor.

Then came the regulatory regime of the New Deal, with the federal government regulating everything from the amount of wheat that farmers could grow to retirement programs in the railroad industry, from wages and working hours to coal industry production, from labor negotiations to the price of almost everything. Today the states are slaves to federal "mandates." They beg for federal dollars to finance the seemingly unlimited regulatory mandates emanating from Washington, D.C., covering how fast citizens may drive, when and how much alcohol they may consume, how to treat drinking water, who may own firearms and where they may use them, and an endless stream of nanny-state harassment. When a state does protest an "unfair" and burdensome federal mandate, it is usually quickly disciplined by the mere threat of diminished federal subsidies for the state politicians' favorite pork-barrel programs, usually for road construction.

The political corruption that the Progressives were concerned about expanded by orders of magnitude thanks to the Seventeenth Amendment. U.S. senators now travel all around the country seeking special-interest campaign contributions; senators from practically every state spend a great deal of time fund-raising in New York and California, for example, because that's where the money is.

Federalism is long dead, despite the Supreme Court's occasional pronouncements to the contrary. Conservatives who celebrate every time the Court seems to allow the states a tiny bit of latitude in organizing their own political affairs might as well be barking at the moon. Rossum was right when he concluded, "The original federal design [of the Constitution] effectively died as a result of the social and political forces that resulted in the adoption of the Seventeenth Amendment."

THE INCOME TAX

Alexander Hamilton, with his disdain for laissez-faire economics, advocated a hyperinterventionist approach that would put the federal government in control of the economy. Feeding the massive central government that he favored would require a healthy diet of revenue (to be taken out of the pockets of citizens and put into the hands of the government in the nation's capital). Hence his calls for excise and sales taxes, a national property tax, prohibitive tariffs, and more. As the historian Clinton Rossiter put it, "Hamilton took a large view of the power of Congress to tax because he took a large view of the power to spend." Recall that Hamilton was so committed to federal taxation that he pushed President Washington to use military force to make Pennsylvanians pay the infamous whiskey tax.

Despite Hamilton's ambitions, the Founding Fathers were careful not to give the federal government expansive powers to tax the people. In fact, under the Articles of Confederation the central government had no taxing powers at all; revenues were raised by the sovereign states. Even under the Constitution, the functions of government were meant to be funded by modest "revenue tariffs" and selected excise taxes; "direct taxes" could be levied only in proportion to each state's population.

The Founding Fathers did not adopt an income tax. Thomas Jefferson made it a point to denounce the notion of income taxation in his first inaugural address, when he said that "a wise and frugal Government . . . *shall not take from the mouth of labor the bread it has earned*" (emphasis added).[20] Jefferson's dictum was an expression of Lockean natural rights theory: the purpose of government, Jefferson believed, was to *protect* these God-given rights to life, liberty, and property, not to take them away from citizens.

Hamilton did not himself call for an income tax, but the sales and excise taxes he championed were not much different from income taxation. Sales and excise taxes are *indirect* taxes on some people's income; excise taxes, for example, render the taxed industries less profitable and thus deplete the incomes of those who work and/or invest in those industries.[21] And as a voracious tax increaser in his day, Hamilton would undoubtedly have approved of the adoption of an income tax as a way to increase the federal government's revenue and centralize its power. Since there was such overwhelming opposition to the notion of taxing income in his day, Hamilton was forced to advocate myriad other forms of taxation instead to fund the more "energetic" government that he desired.

The first federal income tax was introduced in 1862,

during the period of Hamiltonian hegemony, as a war-financing tool. Using the now-familiar principle of "progressive taxation," the government instituted a two-tiered system: incomes up to $10,000 per year were taxed at 3 percent, while income levels above that were taxed at 5 percent.[22] This income tax was abolished in 1872, but the experience had whetted the appetites of special-interest groups. A forty-year crusade to reinstitute the tax would ensue.

A flat-rate income tax was adopted in 1894, but the Supreme Court ruled it unconstitutional a year later because this direct tax was not levied in proportion to state population. The crusade continued and gained an important ally in President Teddy Roosevelt, whose popularity provided a huge boost to the cause. Congressmen from the Midwest and West and Progressive ideologues all joined the cause because their constituents—farmers— had been so disproportionately burdened by the Republican Party's decades-old high tariff policy.

By 1913 a deal had been cut whereby Congress would reduce tariff rates in return for farm state support for an income tax. President Woodrow Wilson convened an emergency session of Congress to push through the income tax and a constitutional amendment authorizing it.[23] The income tax became law on October 3, 1916. The Sixteenth Amendment establishing the tax was very simply worded: "The Congress shall have power to lay and collect taxes on income, from whatever source derived, without apportionment among the several States, and without regard to any census or enumeration." (American farmers would soon regret their support for the government's income tax; by 1930 tariff rates had risen to the highest rates ever—an average of 59.1 percent. Federal politicians realized that with all that income tax revenue coming in, they could afford to enact prohibitive tariffs as a way to buy political support from various manufacturing industries.)

Although dozens of treatises and thousands of scholarly articles have been published on income taxation, one point that is usually either downplayed or ignored altogether is what such taxation meant to the principle of federalism. The income tax, as much as anything else, ended the ability of the citizens of the states to effectively influence their own central government. It centralized power to a degree that even Hamilton himself could hardly have imagined. It gave the federal government virtually unlimited access to funds and allowed it to pry into every business transaction and the records of every working person in America. It diminished the ability of the state and local governments to finance *their* activities and rendered them beggars for whatever crumbs of revenue their rulers in Washington, D.C., decided to throw their way. With federal "grants" (of the taxpayers' own money) to the states, the federal government became more and more in charge of state governments, rendering them mere appendages or franchises of the central government. This was essentially the relationship between the federal government and the states that Hamilton had proposed at the Constitutional Convention more than a century and a quarter earlier.

The income tax was also a complete repudiation of Jefferson's natural rights doctrine. Private property was no longer sacrosanct. The amount of income the citizen might keep would be determined by the "needs" of government. And if the citizen refused to pay his income tax, the government could imprison him and confiscate his wealth to pay the taxes due.

The income tax also helped to achieve the Hamiltonian objective of an almost dictatorial executive branch that controlled billions of dollars. As Frank Chodorov explained in a book on the income tax:

> [T]he Sixteenth Amendment corroded the American concept of natural rights; ultimately reduced the American citizen to a status of subject, so much so that he is not aware of it; enhanced Executive power to the point of reducing Congress to innocuity; and enabled the central government to bribe the states, once independent units, into subservience. No kingship in the history of the world ever exercised more power than our Presidency, or had more of the people's wealth at its disposal.[24]

Chodorov first wrote those words in 1954. More than a half century of additional accumulations of executive power would likely have been unimaginable to him. Hamilton, on the other hand, would certainly be smiling.

The income tax knocked away another vestige of the states' rights system that the founders had designed. The rights of secession and nullification had already been abolished in 1865; citizens who opposed what they believed to be the central government's unconstitutional usurpations of power had to rely on political action, protests, and boycotts as the only powers they had left. What the income tax did was to give the central government vast resources with which to oppose even those feeble attempts by citizens to influence their own governments. A good illustration of this point is made by Chodorov:

Mr. Lincoln had great difficulty in enforcing a moderate form of conscription, even in wartime; now we have peacetime conscription. . . . Mr. Lincoln had difficulty with his draft because he did not have the wherewithal to hire an army of enforcement agents. Thanks to the income tax, our present government is not so handicapped.[25]

Another ominous effect of the tremendous centralization of political power that income taxation has created is government-financed and -enforced mind control. For example:

[T]he farmer who receives checks [from the U.S. Department of Agriculture] for not planting does not realize that his grandfather would have thought the practice immoral; he accepts the taking of gratuities as the regular order of things . . . because government propaganda has got him into that frame of mind.[26]

The same can be said of millions of other individuals and groups that receive government checks or other types of special favors. As the ancient saying goes, "He who takes the king's shilling becomes the king's man."

CENTRAL PLANNING THROUGH
CENTRAL BANKING

The third "shot" in the Revolution of 1913 came with the Federal Reserve Act, which established the Federal Reserve Board. Hamilton can be considered the founding father of central banking in America, and the creation of the Fed is one of his legacies. Indeed, the Fed represents the culmination of Hamilton's plan for government control of the money supply.

Even today the Federal Reserve Board itself points to Hamilton as its institutional parent. A Fed publication entitled "A History of Central Banking in the United States" states that "the Federal Reserve has similarities to the country's first attempt at central banking, and in that regard it owes an intellectual debt to Alexander Hamilton."[27] The publication even trumpets the fact that in one of Hamilton's comments on central banking, written in 1791, he ended up "sounding like a modern-day Fed chairman." This rather self-serving Fed history claims that the Federal Reserve's sole purpose is "to better serve commerce and government" and quickly adds, "That was the inspiration behind Alexander Hamilton's campaign to establish the First Bank of the United States, behind the efforts of the Second Bank and the banking legislation that followed, and the core purpose of the Federal Reserve Act."

As the Fed indicates, Hamilton's plan came in stages: first the Bank of the United States, then the National Currency Acts of the 1860s, and finally the Federal Reserve Act of December 1913. With the Fed, the federal government finally established monopolistic control over the money supply. It meant "the realizing of the hopes of Hamilton and his successors, including Clay and Lincoln," wrote Michael Lind, who celebrates the fact that Americans now live in "Hamilton's Republic."[28]

The story of the creation of the Federal Reserve is the story of a decades-long political crusade by bankers, industrialists (especially those associated with the railroad industry), and power-hungry politicians.

During the late nineteenth and early twentieth centuries the banking industry faced the same issue that many other industries did: too much competition. The National Currency Acts had, in fact, eliminated much of the competition, but state-chartered banks continued to exist despite the acts' imposition of a punitive 10 percent tax on them. As Murray Rothbard wrote, "These state banks, free of the high legal capital requirements that kept entry restricted in national banking, flourished during the 1880s and 1890s and provided stiff competition for the national banks themselves."[29] As with other industries, bankers tried to create voluntary cartels, but cartels are notoriously unstable. So inevitably they turned to government to enforce their cartel for them.

The banks' biggest complaints involved the so-called inelasticity of the money supply—that is, "the national banking system did not provide sufficient room for inflationary expansions of credit by the nation's banks."[30] Banks that issued their own banknotes suffered if they inflated their currency and too many depositors demanded their money, especially if they demanded it in gold. But this "problem" could be overcome if the government became a monopoly issuer of all currency and gave itself the right to legally counterfeit. That is precisely what the Federal Reserve did, and has been doing since 1914. Ever since, if a bank acted irresponsibly and inflated its currency and was short of funds to meet its depositors' demands, the Fed could step in and provide it with more paper money. Banks no longer held reserves in gold; gold was deposited with the Federal Reserve for "safe keeping."

Murray Rothbard summed up how this sweeping change came to pass: "The financial elites of this country . . . were responsible for putting through the Federal Reserve System, as a governmentally created and sanctioned cartel device to enable the nation's banks to inflate the money supply . . . without suffering quick retribution from depositors or noteholders demanding cash."[31]

The crusade for a central bank drew intellectual cover from a number of influential economists and other social scientists. These academics had learned the supposed virtues of collectivism and statism from the so-called German Historical School of economics—which, as the Hamilton idolater Michael Lind correctly notes, traced its lineage to none other than Alexander Hamilton and his followers in America.[32] Oddly enough, Hamilton's ideas had to migrate to Germany before they came back to America's shores, but they were indispensable to the creation of the Federal Reserve. In the first half of the nineteenth century the German intellectual Friedrich List essentially copied Hamilton's ideas and presented them to German university audiences, and his intellectual heirs in the latter half of the century formed the German Historical School. Intellectuals from this school disavowed much of the accumulated knowledge of economics, believing that economic planners could somehow "repeal" the laws of supply and demand and enact price controls, expansionary monetary policy, protectionism, high taxes, and other interventions without harming the economy.[33] This school eventually spread the "doctrine of economic nationalism"—that is, neomercantilism—back to American students and professors.[34]

The American acolytes of the German Historical School's Hamiltonian mercantilism—among them E.R.A. Seligman of Columbia University and Jeremiah Jenks of Cornell University, both close advisers to Teddy Roosevelt—played a key role in the drive for the Federal Reserve. As Rothbard wrote, they lent "the patina of their allegedly scientific expertise to the . . . drive for a central bank. To achieve a regime of big government . . . interests seeking special privilege, and intellectuals offering scholarship and ideology, must work hand in hand."[35]

And work hand in hand they did. These intellectuals and the business elite were united in their support for a central bank, in part because they agreed that America should pursue what Hamilton called "imperial glory," especially after the United States acquired colonies in the Philippines, Cuba, and Puerto Rico. For example, the American Economic Association, whose cofounder Richard T. Ely was one of the most prominent proponents of the German Historical School, got a number of wealthy businessmen to fund a book entitled *Essays in Colonial Finance.*[36] Other publications advocated opening up new markets around the world, by military force if necessary. Protectionism had led to overproduction by domestic manufacturers, who were always on the lookout for ways of dumping their excess products. But if empire had its advantages, according to the economic nationalists, it also came with exorbitant costs; they argued that a central bank was needed, in addition to the income tax, to support these costs.

In the aftermath of a recession in 1907 numerous academic conferences were held calling for a central bank, including three at Columbia University alone, sponsored by E.R.A. Seligman. The *Wall Street Journal* editorialized in favor of a governmental monetary monopoly for years, starting in 1909 with a fourteen-part series entitled "A Central Bank of Issue."[37] Various studies were published by the same cast of characters hailing the alleged superiority of European central banking systems over the American system.

With the intellectual groundwork having been laid, the

Senate's foremost proponent of central banking set to work on legislation in late 1910. On November 22 Senator Nelson Aldrich gathered several of his close allies and sailed off to a private club on Jekyll Island, Georgia, to write up the legislation that would create the Federal Reserve. A year later the American Bankers Association endorsed the bill, which finally became law in December 1913.

The creation of the Fed and the enactment of the income tax amendment, combined with the climate of opinion endorsing the view that America should become an empire and not just a constitutional republic, was the ultimate victory for early twentieth-century Hamiltonians. States' rights were finally abolished altogether; the federal government's greedy hand was permanently implanted into the taxpayers' pockets; and Washington, D.C., finally had a legal counterfeiting monopoly that could be hidden behind the guise of "monetary policy" by clever academics and political activists and pundits.

The immediate results were disastrous for America. These new funding mechanisms allowed Woodrow Wilson to plunge America disastrously into the European war, a war that provided no benefits to America but exacted a tremendous cost in terms of blood and treasure. Like all wars, World War I permanently ratcheted up the powers of government and fueled the urge among politicians to "plan" American society in peacetime just as they had "planned" during the war.

The longer-term results were just as bad. The Fed's monetary expansion during the late 1920s led to the inevitable boom-and-bust cycle, caused by too much cheap credit that enables too many businesses to become overcapitalized. When this happens— that is, when there is more production capacity than is warranted by consumer demand—the only way out is through a liquidation of some of that capital. Such liquidations are what ignited the stock market crash and the Great Depression.[38]

From 1789, the year that the Constitution was ratified, until 1913 the consumer price level in America remained stable, with some swings during the business cycle and during wartime. Since then prices have risen about twenty-fold, even though we have been told for almost a century that the purpose of the Federal Reserve is to ensure price *stability.*

In any event, the Revolution of 1913 was completed by December of that year; Americans have lived in Hamilton's neo-mercantilist republic ever since.

CHAPTER 8

~

The Poisoned Fruits
of "Hamilton's Republic"

Hamilton was the defender of those who already had land and . . . wealth. He wanted these men to stay landed and wealthy and knew that laissez-faire would not do the trick. In order to keep the tops at the top, Hamilton proposed taxes, regulation, central banking—big government. . . . Alexander Hamilton, the first American champion of big business and big government, has won.

—TIMOTHY P. CARNEY, *THE BIG RIPOFF:
HOW BIG BUSINESS AND BIG GOVERNMENT
STEAL YOUR MONEY*

It is indeed true that Americans now live in Hamilton's Republic. Many liberals delight in this fact. That is not surprising; after all, Hamilton was the godfather of economic interventionism and big government. But many conservatives embrace Hamilton as well. That might seem odd on its face, but the fact is that the *real* Hamilton has remained largely hidden from view in most historical treatments. Conservatives who genuinely believe in limited government are not generally exposed to the Hamilton who at the

Constitutional Convention called for a kinglike permanent president and who subsequently dedicated himself to *undermining* the limits on governmental power laid out in the very Constitution he championed in *The Federalist Papers.* So-called neoconservatives, meanwhile, tend to revere Hamilton precisely because he so brilliantly undermined the Jeffersonian principles of limited government and established a political template for the pursuit of "national greatness" and "imperial glory" through big government.

But no matter how many contemporary historians, politicians, and pundits celebrate Hamilton's influence, the fact is that his political legacy has been largely a curse on America, not a blessing. Many of America's economic and political achievements for which neo-Hamiltonian writers often credit Hamilton have often occurred *despite* rather than because of the adoption of his principal ideas—centralized governmental bureaucracy, public debt, business-government "partnerships," protectionism, heavy taxation and regulation, monetary manipulation through central banking, and corporate welfare. Moreover, many of the disasters of American history have their roots in Hamilton's philosophy of centralized governmental power combined with mercantilist economics. This would include not only the War between the States, which claimed more than 600,000 American lives, but also the massive political corruption that followed the war, the U.S. government's imperialist bent that began in the late nineteenth century with the Spanish-American War, the destruction of constitutional government by activist federal judges, the invasive tyranny of the IRS, our gargantuan national debt, and the monetary expansion and economic interventionism that led to the Great Depression. And this is only a partial list.

Indeed, as soon as Hamiltonianism snuffed out Jeffersonian-ism for good in 1913, President Woodrow Wilson was free to foolishly plunge America into the "Great War" in Europe. Wilson had campaigned on a promise to keep America out of the European war, and had states' rights still existed in America, it is unlikely that he would have been able to rally support for the intervention. (As the historians Thomas Woods and Kevin R. C. Gutzman wrote, "Even the worst outrage Germany perpetrated against the United States—the 1915 sinking of the *Lusitania,* the famous British ocean liner, killing some 128 Americans on board—provoked very few calls for American intervention in the war."[1]) Wilson's senseless intervention not only cost the lives of more than 100,000 Americans but also ended up strengthening the hands of both the Russian Communists and the Nazis in Germany.[2] As Jim Powell convincingly demonstrated in his book *Wilson's War,* had Wilson not gotten America involved in World War I, there probably would not have been a World War II.

We have, ever since the early twentieth century, been burdened with the highly centralized governmental power of which Alexander Hamilton was the first and greatest champion. Hamilton, of course, is not responsible for every individual action that politicians and bureaucrats have undertaken in the two centuries since his death. But he failed to heed the ancient wisdom that monopolistic government would inevitably lead to tyranny, corruption, and foolish if not destructive economic interventionism. That is Hamilton's curse.

CORPORATE WELFARE RUN AMOK

The name that neo-Hamiltonians give to corporate welfare policies, "economic nationalism," is a sham. Hamiltonian "business-government partnerships," as we have seen, use the coercive powers of the state to benefit a small group of Americans (politically connected businesses) at the expense of a much larger group of Americans (consumers and competing companies). In today's world, neo-Hamiltonian mercantilism has run amok with almost too many "business-government partnerships" to count.

One of the latest analyses of neo-Hamiltonian mercantilism is Timothy P. Carney's *The Big Ripoff: How Big Business and Big Government Steal Your Money*, published in 2006.[3] Carney recognizes the Hamiltonian roots of what he calls "the big myth"— that "big business and big government are rivals—that big business wants small government."[4] In fact, big business (and some small and medium-sized ones too) has long been closely tied to the state, exactly as Hamilton wanted. Remember Hamilton's scheme to attach the wealthy to the government by turning them into government bondholders, or by any other trick he could think of.

Carney provides hundreds of examples of how big business and big government collaborate to plunder the rest of America; a few of them illustrate how pervasive this corrupt system has been for a long, long time:

- Big business supported FDR's Social Security taxes because it understood that the taxes would impose a disproportionate burden on their smaller competitors and place them at a competitive disadvantage.

- After World War II the much-heralded Marshall Plan was essentially a giant grant of corporate welfare for American corporations that did little to help with Europe's postwar economic recovery.

- President Eisenhower oversaw the building of the Interstate Highway System, which was the biggest pork-barrel project in American history. Today the U.S. Department of Transportation still uses "highway grants" as a way of doling out more than $10 billion per year in corporate welfare.

- Major business groups supported President Nixon's imposition of disastrous wage and price controls, in return, no doubt, for subsidies of all types from the administration.

- When President Gerald Ford proposed tax and spending *cuts,* he was denounced by major business leaders, such as Salomon Brothers, the Wall Street firm that made a fortune marketing the federal government's bonds.

- President Carter was endorsed by the *New York Post* in 1980, a few days after his administration granted a subsidy to Rupert Murdoch, owner of the paper.

- Carter also created the U.S. Department of Energy, which distributes more than $5 billion in corporate welfare each year.

- President Reagan granted the ethanol industry tens of millions of dollars in corporate welfare, enacted protectionist trade policies in several industries, and *increased* federal taxes in 1986 by signing a law that eliminated almost all federal tax exemptions and deductions. He had the support of the big business community, which can be easily bought off with promises of individual tax breaks or subsidies.

- President George H. W. Bush endorsed various protectionist trade policies, in the long tradition of the Republican

Party, and did nothing to end billions of dollars annually in corporate welfare from myriad government programs. President Clinton had a similar record.

- President George W. Bush imposed 50 percent steel industry tariffs and created hundreds of billions of dollars in profits for the pharmaceutical industry by further socializing the Medicare prescription drug benefit, among other things. The war in Iraq transferred tens of billions of dollars to American corporate contractors of all sorts.[5]

To understand the absurdity of referring to these neo-Hamiltonian corporate welfare schemes as "economic nationalism," consider one such program, the federal government's subsidies to cotton farmers. Government policy maintains that if the price of cotton on the world market falls below 52 cents per pound, the government will use taxpayer dollars to subsidize cotton farmers for the difference between the world price and 52 cents. In 2005 American cotton farmers had a record year, thanks to perfect weather conditions and the eradication of the dreaded boll weevil; a Texas cotton farmer named Eugene Bednarz, for example, harvested an incredible 4,000 bales of cotton.[6] But the record supply of cotton also helped to drop the world price to 35 cents. So the U.S. government wrote Mr. Bednarz a check for $340,000 to cover the difference in price—or put more accurately, for doing absolutely nothing. Neither consumers nor taxpayers received anything in return for that expenditure of tax dollars. It was a pure transfer—legal plunder—from the taxpayers to Bednarz and hundreds of other cotton farmers. Texas cotton farmers alone pocketed $637.5 million in such subsidies in 2005.[7]

There are countless other examples of how corporate welfare

works, as Carney shows. The federal government guarantees sugar farmers—mostly large corporate farms—a price of 18 cents per pound and provides other, indirect forms of corporate welfare by building canals and dikes, dredging lakes for the farmers at taxpayers' expense, and giving below-market-rate loans.[8]

The federal government's Overseas Private Investment Corporation (OPIC) subsidizes exports of American products. These products include everything from Ritz Hotels to oil to agricultural products to weapons.

Then there is the Export-Import Bank, which extends low-interest loans to foreign countries with the contingency that they use the money to purchase American products. Simply writing checks to corporations can be politically dangerous, so the government has conceived of various ruses, like this one, to keep the public in the dark. But this money ends up in the coffers of American corporations, and American taxpayers, who foot the bill, get nothing at all. Even worse, some foreign loans are for American corporations to build factories overseas, at the expense of building those same factories at home. And it is all spoken of as being charitable "foreign aid" to the downtrodden of the world.[9]

Cato Institute researchers have estimated very conservatively that the federal government dishes out at least $90 billion per year in corporate welfare of one form or another.[10] And that's just the result of direct expenditures; regulations and taxes that impose disproportionate economic burdens on smaller competitors would probably be impossible to measure. Protectionism, too, would add additional billions per year to the Cato Institute's estimates.

The federal government is not the only source of corporate welfare, of course. Most egregiously, local governments use the power of "eminent domain" to condemn private residential property so it can be sold (at fire-sale prices) to corporations or real estate developers. The local governments' property tax revenue then increases, which supposedly justifies this naked (legalized) theft of private property.[11]

Eminent domain (which means "superior ownership") was originally supposed to be used to acquire property "for public uses" such as roads, schools, or hospitals. But in politicians' hunger for more and more tax revenue—and for corporate campaign contributions—they have perverted the law to allow condemnation of land for *private* use. This is not how local politicians describe it, however. They call it "urban redevelopment" or some other euphemism for "the common good." It's a localized version of "national greatness" rhetoric. America today is awash in neo-Hamiltonian mercantilism in the form of corporate welfare.

JUDICIAL MONARCHY

Though Hamilton fought for adoption of the Constitution, he did not, of course, pay much heed to what the document actually *said*. Despite the precise language the framers used to outline the narrow range of powers granted to the federal government, Hamilton suddenly claimed that there were "implied" and "resulting" powers of government. This was his way of trying to give the federal government a blank check to expand its powers. It was the exact opposite of Jefferson's strict constructionist views, but over the long term Hamilton's viewpoint would prevail. As we have seen, he was helped by his Federalist allies on the bench, especially Chief Justice John Marshall, who did their best to implement this view, and by other jurists who have followed their lead ever since.

This was the Hamiltonian judicial revolution. Hamilton argued in *Federalist* no. 78 that the judiciary was the "least dangerous" branch of government, but in fact, because he succeeded in pushing his judicial philosophy, he has made the American people the subjects of judicial tyranny. Americans today no longer live under a Constitution at all but are ruled by the arbitrary and often contradictory opinions of governmental lawyer/bureaucrats that invariably lead to more governmental power and less freedom.[12]

The Hamiltonian judicial revolution began in earnest in the 1930s. Between 1937 and 1995 the U.S. Supreme Court did not rule a single piece of federal legislation to be unconstitutional. There were no checks at all on the powers of government—exactly as Hamilton would have wanted it.[13] To give the federal government a blank check, the Court adopted the amazing line of argument that the government needed to prove not that any of its programs were *actually* legitimate under the Constitution, only that they were "hypothetically legitimate."[14] Of course, any reasonably clever lawyer can dream up myriad hypothetical situations to justify virtually any kind of governmental action.

During the 1930s the Supreme Court became "FDR's rubber stamp," wrote the legal scholar Kevin R. C. Gutzman.[15] It did so by reversing decades of previous Supreme Court precedents with creative language. Notably, in 1937 the Court suddenly "discovered" that a voluntary contract between employers and employees wasn't always really a contract and should not therefore be protected by the Constitution's Contract Clause, which prohibits state interference in legal, private contracts. That is how the Court declared a federal minimum wage law to be legal and constitutional, even though it was a crystal-clear example of the state's interfering with, not protecting, freedom of contract.[16] Earlier courts had ruled against minimum-wage legislation.

Similarly, the Court began declaring that almost any kind of human behavior had some kind of relationship to interstate commerce and that therefore the federal government had the right to regulate that behavior under the Constitution's Commerce Clause. Recall that Hamilton himself was probably the first to expand the definition of the Commerce Clause in this way. He insisted that a legislature empowered to "regulate commerce" was not limited to merely regulating interstate tariffs, as others had supposed. To Hamilton, the Commerce Clause created the "implied power" to "police, tax, and encourage . . . all those undertakings covered by the words 'trade,' 'manufacturing,' 'finance,' and even 'agriculture.'"[17] In justifying his claim that the federal government had the "implied power" to regulate commerce *within* every state, he asked in his *Opinion as to the Constitutionality of the Bank of the United States,* "What regulation of commerce does not extend to the internal commerce of every State?"[18]

Jefferson mocked Hamilton's twisted reasoning in an 1800 letter to Edward Livingston, saying, "Congress . . . [is] authorized to defend the nation. Ships are necessary for defence; copper is necessary for ships; mines necessary for copper; a company necessary to work mines; and who can doubt this reasoning who has ever played at 'This is the House that Jack Built'? Under such a process of filiation of necessities the sweeping clause makes clean work."[19] It is fair to say that for several generations now the U.S. Supreme Court has been hard at work playing the very game that

Jefferson mocked, using the Commerce Clause to make "clean work" of expanding the central government's powers.

The largest source of Supreme Mischief is what legal scholars call "the Hamiltonian interpretation" of the Constitution's General Welfare Clause.[20] This interpretation says that Congress can *enact any law* that it believes will advance "the general welfare"—as defined by Congress, of course. Hamilton had proposed this broad interpretation at the Constitutional Convention, but it was rejected. The framers accepted what is known as the "Madisonian interpretation," which is the strict constructionist theory that Congress can do nothing more than vote to *spend tax dollars,* as designated by the Constitution's *enumerated powers.* Nevertheless, Hamilton triumphed in the end, thanks to the Supreme Court.

The Court, in fact, has interpreted the General Welfare Clause more broadly than even Hamilton could have imagined. In the late 1930s Congress passed several pieces of agricultural legislation in response to the Supreme Court's invalidation of the Agricultural Adjustment Act of 1933. In doing so, Congress embraced the Hamiltonian interpretation of the General Welfare Clause by stating that the clause "is not limited by the subsequently enumerated powers."[21] These laws still exist today; the Hamiltonian position was never challenged thereafter. Ever since, the only limitation to congressional spending is the imaginations of politicians and lobbyists—and the depth of the taxpayers' pockets. Indeed, the job of every Washington lobbyist is to concoct arguments that what is really in the narrow private interests of themselves or their clients is really in "the national interest" and therefore serves "the general welfare."

Ever since states' rights essentially died in 1913, the citizens of the states have had no real ability to challenge the constitutionality of federal legislation. That's why not a single federal law was ruled unconstitutional by the Supreme Court for almost sixty years. The state governments have become pathetic beggars, with a puppy dog penchant for sitting, standing, barking—whatever the federal government wants—in return for "federal grants."

Actually "federal grants" are a matter of (1) the federal government confiscating funds from the taxpayers of the respective states, and (2) giving a few crumbs back, not to the taxpayers, but to state and local *politicians,* who then use the funds to buy votes for themselves with highway construction contracts, school construction contracts, and other forms of corporate welfare and pork-barrel spending. With federal grants, state and local politicians feel like they are getting something for nothing: they can buy votes with pork-barrel spending without having to raise taxes. (Or at least, they don't have to raise *local* or *state* taxes, which would get them in trouble with voters. The federal government may raise taxes to pay for the spending, but local politicians can wash their hands of it even though the federal tax affects their constituents.)

The bribery power inherent in federal grants allows the federal government to regulate behavior at the state and local levels even if it does not have constitutional authorization to do so. For example:

> In 1985, Nevada passed a law that increased its speed limit to 70 mph. The law also provided that if the federal officials threatened to cut off aid to the state, the limit was to be lowered. *Within sixty seconds of the new law coming into effect,* the Chief of the Nevada division of the

Federal Highway Administration advised that the federal Department of Transportation declared that all future funds for state highways would be withheld unless the Nevada speed limit was reduced to 55 mph. (emphasis added)[22]

Nevada was forced to retain the 55-mph speed limit.

When Congress passed the National Minimum Drinking Age Act in 1984, making it illegal for anyone under twenty-one years of age to drink alcohol, South Dakota challenged the law as a violation of the Twenty-first Amendment to the Constitution, which gives the states the power to regulate the sale of liquor. The mere threat of withdrawing federal funds from the state was all it took to defeat South Dakota's protest. The Supreme Court rubber-stamped the federal government's strong-arm tactics, saying it was a legitimate exercise of Congress's spending powers.[23] It is illegal to bribe federal bureaucrats and politicians, but according to the Supreme Court, federal bureaucrats and politicians are free to bribe state and local officials.

Neo-Hamiltonian jurists have also snuffed out states' rights by proclaiming that the Bill of Rights applied to the states as well as to the federal government. This is called the "incorporation doctrine."[24] It runs contrary to the Constitution and its history. The Bill of Rights was intended to limit the power of the federal government, period. But political activists who are appointed as federal judges have made an end run around the constitutional amendment process by simply declaring that the Bill of Rights should also apply to the states. This was originally done in the name of allowing the federal government to protect minority rights, and no one could argue that some good was not done by this. Even some libertarians support the incorporation doctrine because it *has* been used at times to protect liberty. They tend to ignore completely, however, that it has also been used to aggrandize the state *at the expense of individual liberty*.[25] In fact, it has greatly expanded the federal government's nanny-state proclivities to centrally plan everyone's life, business, and behavior.

Neo-Hamiltonians applaud this increased regulatory power, of course. One liberal legal scholar, for instance, celebrates "our secret constitution"—that is, leftist judges' tortured reinterpretations of the Constitution. The Columbia University law professor George P. Fletcher claims that the liberal rewriting of the Constitution via "constitutional law" is the result of self-anointed judges who have decided to discard the Constitution in favor of what they personally regard as "a higher law."[26] If this sounds like judicial dictatorship, that's because it is.

America has been "reinvented," Fletcher approvingly states, thanks to Supreme Court judicial activism. "Truth and justice must prevail over legalistic formalities" like the Constitution, he says.[27] Moreover, he claims that those who "fight" in the name of a "higher law" are allowed "to sidestep the rules."[28] This of course depends on who gets to define what "higher law" means. In reality, this argument is another version of Hamilton's "common good" philosophy.

Fletcher says this "higher law" informed the Republican Party in the post-1865 era—the era of Hamiltonian hegemony— and he is right: the Republicans held a virtual monopoly on power for some fifty years after the war and could define "the common good" or "the higher law" any way that they wanted. The purpose of all of this, writes Fletcher, was to "strengthen the powers of government" and to achieve "the consolidation of the United States as a nation"—to give it more energy, as Hamilton would say.[29]

To Thomas Jefferson, the American Revolution transferred sovereignty from the King of England to the American people. The people were to express that sovereignty as members of distinct political communities organized at the state and local levels. Today the people are not sovereign over their federal government; their federal government is sovereign over them. Much—perhaps most—of the people's sovereignty has been assumed by nine unelected government lawyers with lifetime tenure. No wonder lawyers like Fletcher praise such an outcome. To a large extent, today's statists do not need to get involved with messy democratic politics if they can rely on like-minded government lawyers instead. That is why the political battles over Supreme Court appointees have become so vicious. Hamilton the monarchist never had much trust in the American people, and his political heirs have long been in control of the governmental apparatus in America.

EXECUTIVE DICTATORSHIP

Hamilton expressed his monarchism most clearly in his plan, presented at the Constitutional Convention, for a permanent president who would appoint all the governors of the states and have veto power over all state legislation. While he did not persuade his fellow delegates of his plan for an American king, Hamiltonians have subsequently prevailed in installing monopolistic executive power, just as they have won out in so many other areas.

The framers of the Constitution intended the president to

be the chief executive officer of a relatively small bureaucracy with tightly enumerated powers. From the very beginning of the republic, however, there was a Hamiltonian/Jeffersonian battle over executive power, with the Hamiltonians, of course, advocating more and more power. This power grew as political patronage expanded, allowing the executive branch to buy more and more political supporters. But it was not until the Lincoln administration—and all of its abuses of power (documented in Chapter 6)—that the American president was transformed into a Caesar.[30] The War between the States led to a great centralization of power, and that power was immediately used to accomplish the Hamiltonian agenda of economic nationalism and to promote the long-held New England belief of American "exceptionalism."[31]

After Lincoln's assassination, as Clyde Wilson explains, the president "was now the martyred savior in the world historical drama of American uniqueness."[32] A huge literature developed that depicted Lincoln as a Christ figure who died for America's sins, and "the conflation of America with God's plan for the perfection of human history was complete."[33] "By the time we get to [President Bill] Clinton," writes Wilson, "the imperial office itself had become the object of worship. It does not matter how tainted the credentials of its occupant. In the drama of salvation, a sleazy prevaricator can be the savior of the oppressed. It does not matter if this requires the murder of innocent women and children at home or abroad. The emperor can do no wrong."[34]

The deification of the presidency itself was necessary to achieve Hamilton's dual objectives of "national greatness" and "imperial glory." The Yale University professor David Gelernter, in a book entitled *Americanism: The Fourth Great Western Religion*, argues that ever since Lincoln, Americans have "worshipped" this new "religion" of Americanism and have used it to justify entering various wars around the world, from the Spanish-American War to World War I, to the war in Iraq in 2003.[35]

The president can now enter a war without the consent of Congress, even though the Constitution requires a formal congressional declaration of war; can claim "executive privilege" whenever Congress or anyone else requests that he make public deliberations that are in the public interest; and can issue executive orders to do pretty much anything he chooses, including suspending all constitutional rights of American citizens by arbitrarily declaring them to be "enemy combatants," and supervising the social engineering of all aspects of life, from cradle to grave.[36] Some good things can be done with executive orders, of course, but they represent an assault on the separation of powers and thus on our liberty. Executive orders allow presidents to assume the role of dictator with regard to certain policies.

Hamilton may not have personally approved of this outcome, but it is the end result of the type of government that he favored and that his political heirs have adopted.

ECONOMIC ABUSE

Another key part of Hamilton's legacy is the economic instability that his policies of centralization and taxation have caused. From the beginning he was, as we have seen, the great champion of statism, and he made his case most explicitly in his calls for a national bank.

The logical consequence of Hamiltonian statism was the creation of the Federal Reserve Board. As the Fed itself proudly pronounces, Hamilton was the founding father of central banking

in America, and ultimately economists greatly influenced by
Hamilton himself provided the intellectual cover for the creation
of the Fed. Of course, the Fed's manipulation of the money supply
has created the boom-and-bust cycle that periodically afflicts
America.

Modern economic research has shown that the Fed has
made numerous attempts to create a "political business cycle,"
basically by using its powers over the money supply to pump up
the economy with easy credit just before presidential elections.
The economist Robert Weintraub documented how Fed monetary policy shifted to fit the preferences of newly elected presidents in 1953, 1961, 1969, 1974, and 1977—all years in which
the presidency changed hands.[37] The policy was based, in other
words, not on what was best for the cause of economic growth and
stability but on the Fed chairman's desire to please his boss.
Remember, the Fed chairman, the head of a supposedly independent government agency, is appointed by the president. So taking
such steps might be politically prudent for the Fed chairman and
advantageous to the administration. But they will damage the
nation as a whole, since these tactics generate a perpetual boom-
and-bust cycle.

For example, President Dwight Eisenhower feared that
inflation was a threat and publicly called for slower growth in the
money supply, which was largely controlled by Fed policy. The
money supply grew at the slowest pace in a decade during his
administration, according to Weintraub's research. When Lyndon
Johnson wanted the Fed to step up the pace of its legalized counterfeiting operations to finance both the Vietnam War and a
greatly enlarged welfare state, the Fed saw to it that the money
supply grew more than twice as fast as it had during the Kennedy

administration. These wildly varying rates of monetary growth all took place under the auspices of the same Fed chairman, William McChesney Martin.

Martin's successor, Arthur Burns, was known as a conservative and a staunch supporter of President Richard Nixon. When Burns's staff informed him in the fall of 1972 that the money supply was expected to grow three to four times faster than it had grown during the Johnson administration—an incredibly inflationary, and economically destabilizing, rate—he advocated *even faster* monetary growth to assure Nixon's reelection.[38] And it apparently worked.

The Fed during the Nixon regime created what at the time was considered to be a dangerously high rate of inflation, so President Ford publicly called for slower monetary growth. Burns faithfully complied, currying favor with his new boss. But when Democrat Jimmy Carter replaced President Ford and expressed his desire for even faster monetary growth to finance an enlarged welfare state, Burns complied with him, too, almost doubling the rate of growth of money put into circulation.

The same pattern of behavior has been observed with other Fed chairmen up to the present day. Anyone who is reading this and can recall seeing Fed chairman Alan Greenspan ceremoniously seated next to Hillary Clinton at one of President Clinton's State of the Union speeches now knows why that seemingly strange scene occurred.

In recent years, the Fed has been responsible for the NASDAQ crash and the bursting of the housing market "bubble." In each instance, the Fed first made credit very inexpensive (low interest rates) and widely available. Businesses and individuals then went into debt much more than was prudent. In the former case, too many businesses became capitalized before they even demonstrated that there was a significant consumer market for their products. Cheap credit, courtesy of the Fed, allowed them to do so. A liquidation of billions of dollars of capital ensued. In the case of the housing market, the extraordinarily low interest rates that the Fed orchestrated from late 2001 to 2006 caused many thousands of ordinary citizens to become real estate speculators, overinvesting in real estate that they thought would never drop in price. This was on top of all the "professional" investors who did the same thing. When the real estate market slowed, and then declined, in 2006 and 2007, many of these investors found themselves deep in debt that they could not afford, and mortgage defaults and bankruptcies ballooned as the entire economy teetered on recession.

The legacy of a politicized monetary system is damaging enough, but it is not the only element of Hamilton's statism for which we are paying the price today. Hamilton was, without exaggeration, the nation's first abusive tax collector: the man who helped President Washington organize an army of some 13,000 tax collectors to drag a couple of dozen hapless Pennsylvanians all the way across that state, in winter, to a kangaroo court trial in Philadelphia, and who wanted to hang them all for protesting the piddling whiskey tax.

It is thus fitting that Hamilton's statue in Washington, D.C., adorns the front of the U.S. Treasury Department, which oversees the Internal Revenue Service (IRS). In the same zealous spirit of coercion and intimidation that Hamilton pursued the whiskey tax rebels, the modern-day IRS goes about its business.

As the investigative journalist James Bovard has documented, the IRS "hypocritically requires mistake-free returns when its own books are in shambles. It demands exorbitant sums of money without regard to the accuracy of its claims. It doesn't hesitate to use every possible legal maneuver to get what it wants, sometimes destroying businesses—and lives—in the process."[39] Also, Bovard showed, the General Accounting Office (now known as the Government Accountability Office) discovered that the IRS made more than 20 million unjustified changes to tax returns in one year. These resulted in millions of wrongful demands for even more money from taxpayers, many of which individuals complied with, since there's such pervasive fear of running afoul of the IRS.[40] In addition, the IRS seizes property to sell for "delinquent" taxes even when it sends the tax bills to the wrong address, and it employs an army of informants to snitch on their neighbors and coworkers.[41] It conducts "economic reality audits" by going through taxpayers' personal effects such as their clothing and personal spending records. In general it assumes that citizens have no right to financial privacy.

Hamilton wanted a standing army of tax collectors, and America got one when the internal revenue bureaucracy was created during the Lincoln regime.

ECONOMIC DEPENDENCY

Hamilton also succeeded in his gambit of tying affluent Americans to the federal government in order to ensure the government's growth. It is with the growth of the central government in mind that he championed the national debt and increased taxation of the general public; the bondholders would support tax increases to assure that they got their money back.

Hamilton's political heirs turned the game into a fine art.

During the Lincoln administration the patronage of the federal government skyrocketed thanks to the building of the transcontinental railroads. During World War I government and business collaborated to produce war materials, and like all such efforts, the effort generally resulted in the creation of great wealth for politically connected businesses at the expense of the rest of society, which was forced to pay monopolistic prices for myriad goods and services. More of the same came about during the Great Depression, as the First New Deal attempted to cartelize manufacturing and agriculture. The support of big business for big government was cemented into place by World War I and the First New Deal.

In his book *Hamilton's Republic,* Michael Lind includes Presidents Franklin Roosevelt and Lyndon Johnson in his pantheon of Hamiltonian political figures. "After FDR," he writes, "Lyndon Baines Johnson . . . did the most to implement a version of . . . democratic Hamiltonianism."[42] This is correct in one important sense: the welfare state programs introduced by FDR and Johnson attached millions of Americans to the central government, creating a permanent voting bloc in favor of ever-increasing government. Hamilton wanted to tie affluent bondholders to government to assure their support for its perpetual expansion; his political heirs have succeeded in tying millions of others to the growth of the state—more than half the entire population, in fact. According to the economist Gary Shilling, *52.6 percent* of Americans in 2007 received significant assistance of some kind from the federal government.[43]

The pathologies created by these dependencies are well known and well documented: destruction of the work ethic; family breakup; millions of people trapped in poverty, since taking a job would mean losing thousands of dollars in government benefits; complete dependency on the state. Poverty in America became much worse as soon as government declared "war" on it in the 1960s, at which point it had been in decline for twenty years. Hamilton's notion of tying the people to the government had also created an entire class of people, millions strong, who depend on the federal government.[44] No wonder one historian has called Hamilton the "American Machiavelli."[45]

A MERCANTILIST EMPIRE

Hamiltonianism now involves international as well as domestic corporate welfare of various forms. It began in the late nineteenth and early twentieth centuries, when many American manufacturing industries were "protected" from international competition with high tariffs—precisely as Hamilton advocated in his writings. This protectionism led to artificially inflated prices. But at the same time American manufacturers were striving to achieve "economies of scale"—declining costs per unit of production that come with a larger volume of production. Consequently they were producing much more than could be sold in American markets. The unsold surpluses in turn led to calls by business leaders to "open up" foreign markets for their products.[46] For example, Francis Thurber, president of the U.S. Export Association, declared in 1899, "We must have a place to dump our surplus, which otherwise will constantly depress prices and compel the shutting down of our mills . . . and changing our profits into losses."[47] Other prominent American manufacturers, including Andrew Carnegie, made similar pleas. "Over time," wrote the historian Joseph

Stromberg, "more and more influential men in government and business came to see the securing of foreign markets as the best fix of all."[48]

Foreign markets would be "secured" by the U.S. government, using military force when necessary. The idea was, as Stromberg explained, that "by socializing the costs of finding, opening, and securing foreign markets through an active foreign policy, the U.S. government would guarantee prosperity."[49] The U.S. government pursued the path of mercantilist empire, in other words. As a result, the United States now has a military presence in more than a hundred countries.

The effects of an international mercantilist empire are basically the same as those of a domestic empire, only larger. Mercantilist empires benefit politically connected businesses and industries and aggrandize the state, at the expense of the rest of society. Felix Morley noted several important features of "democratic empires" in his 1959 book, *Freedom and Federalism*.[50] First there is conquest, such as the American conquest of the Philippines and other territories. This leads to "territorial aggrandizement," which is followed by the creation of military alliances to protect the conquered territory.[51] Military alliances become a drain on the treasury, as allies must be constantly subsidized/bribed.

Morley identified other characteristics of empires, including the belief that there should be no debate over foreign policy. Such debate is said to be "unpatriotic."[52] A good contemporary example of this phenomenon would be how *National Review* magazine, which had become a mouthpiece for the Bush administration, in April 2003 ran a cover story entitled "Unpatriotic Conservatives" (written by the former Bush administration speechwriter David Frum) about certain conservatives who had expressed doubts over the wisdom of invading Iraq in 2003. The article was subtitled "A War Against America."

The final characteristic of empires, according to Morley, is that they are sold to the public in grandiose terms about spreading blessings for all mankind, when in reality their main purpose is to allow those who pull the strings of the empire to accumulate money and power. The American empire is merely Hamiltonian mercantilism on a grand scale. As with all empires, the citizens tend to be the servants rather than the masters of their own government.

CONCLUSION

~

Ending the Curse

[T]here are far too many great men in the world;
there are too many legislators, organizers, . . . con-
ductors of the people, fathers of nations, etc.
—Frédéric Bastiat, *The Law*

M ichael Lind has written that "it is the Hamiltonians who
have won the major struggles to determine what kind of
country the United States would be."[1] Aside from the fact that Lind
haphazardly equates the "country" with the *government*—a mistake
many commentators make as they overstate the importance of politics—his point is entirely valid. In fact, it is difficult to pinpoint any
of Hamilton's ideas that have *not* prevailed over Jefferson's.

Remember, true federalism has been dead for more than a
century. The states have become mere puppet governments controlled by their masters in Washington. Americans endure pervasive and confiscatory taxation. We have long had an imperial
presidency. American foreign policy seeks a version of Hamilton's
"imperial glory," dressed up in various guises, such as "promoting
global democracy." Hamilton's standing army of tax collectors
exists in the form of the IRS. Mercantilistic economic interventionism has replaced real capitalism, for the most part. Americans
are buried in an avalanche of public debt that is hardly the

"blessing" Hamilton promised; the unfunded obligations of the federal government alone amount to more than $70 *trillion,* which would require an average tax rate of more than 80 percent to pay off.[2] Hamiltonian judicial activists beginning with John Marshall have rewritten (read: abandoned) the Constitution to make that document what Hamilton wanted it to be: a rubber stamp for approving almost any governmental activity imaginable. And America has a powerful central bank, the Federal Reserve, that has instigated economic boom-and-bust cycles and prevented a free market from operating in the banking industry.

In short, Hamiltonian statism reigns. The only reason America has prospered in the face of this monopolistic government Leviathan is that this country has such vast resources, including what the economist Julian Simon has called "the ultimate resource"—people—and a relatively high degree of economic freedom compared to the rest of the world.

But Ronald Reagan was right: government is usually the problem, not the solution, when it comes to the big issues of peace and prosperity.

So what can be done? How can we end Hamilton's curse?

RECLAIMING OUR RIGHTS

If Americans are ever to have more peace and prosperity and less government, it is imperative that a *devolution of power* occur. Americans need to reclaim their rights under the Ninth and Tenth Amendments of the Constitution to begin restoring the American tradition of states' rights as a means of controlling their own government. Some form of legal and peaceful resistance to the central state must come into existence once again.

This would require a return to the *American* tradition of states' rights. Until 1865, Americans from all regions of the country assumed the responsibility *themselves* for determining the constitutionality (or unconstitutionality) of federal laws and regulations. They did not buy into the notion that the most important questions relating to their liberties should be decided by one man, the chief justice of the United States, and four of his political compatriots on the Supreme Court. That may have been John Marshall's ideal, but it was not the ideal of a vast number of Americans, including such figures as President Andrew Jackson, who essentially ignored the Court's decision on the constitutionality of the Bank of the United States.

A first step toward returning to the states' rights tradition would be to revive the Jeffersonian idea of interposition—that is, of the citizens of the states deciding for themselves, through their local political representatives, issues of constitutionality. Similarly, the Jeffersonian principle of nullification must be revived if Americans are ever again to become the masters rather than the servants of their own government.[3] In the first half of the nineteenth century citizens of all regions of the country expressed their refusal to abide by the federal government's unconstitutional usurpations of power by having their state and local political representatives issue ordinances of nullification. In the spirit of Jefferson's Kentucky Resolve of 1798, these laws announced that the citizens of the free, independent, and sovereign states would not submit to any whim of the federal government if their rights were threatened. That was back in the pre-1865 era when consent of the governed still existed in America and no politician had yet dreamed of abolishing that consent by force of arms.

Power needs to be stripped away from the federal judiciary and returned to the people. So-called judicial review has resulted only in judicial tyranny, or government by judiciary. Americans cannot lean on the naive hope that the federal judiciary will someday be dominated by devotees of individual liberty. More than two hundred years of history have shown that the federal judiciary almost invariably expands federal power and perks. And with most American law schools still training grounds for leftist judicial activism—that is, for the rewriting of the Constitution that Hamilton pioneered with his notion of "implied powers"—there is little chance that the federal judiciary will make an abrupt shift now. That is why there must be a devolution of power away from the federal judiciary in particular and the federal government in general.

The American political system must also be "unrigged" in order to allow competition by third parties. As it stands now, the two major political parties have established laws and regulations that make it impossible for any significant competition to materialize. For example, in many states, third-party candidates for Congress must gather ten thousand or more signatures in order to be placed on the ballot. No such restrictions apply to the Democratic and Republican candidates.

This is essential, for there are still a few statesmen left in America who are articulate defenders of limited, constitutional government. Congressman Ron Paul of Texas is the most obvious example. Congressman Paul ran for the Republican Party nomination for president in 2007, and his popularity—especially among younger Americans—enabled him to out-fund-raise even Hillary Clinton for much of that period. He garnered more votes in the early primaries and caucuses than onetime front-runner Mayor Rudy Giuliani and other Republican hopefuls. But the establishment and its media accomplices never gave Congressman Paul a fair hearing.

Once the voting began on the day of the New Hampshire primary, not a single television network invited him on the air for an interview—something the networks had routinely done before the election got serious and the votes began to be counted.

Congressman Paul challenged the regime by openly criticizing the very existence of the Federal Reserve and even the federal income tax. For this, he was censored by the major parties and their literary lapdogs, the mainstream media, despite his huge popularity and his fund-raising successes. He was not running as a third-party candidate, as he had done before, but the effect was the same: anyone who challenges the status quo in Hamilton's Republic is beaten down by the political and media elite.

This must end if Hamilton's curse is ever to be lifted and if America is ever again to be "the land of the free." Citizens must take matters into their own hands and vote out of office anyone who opposes fair and open competition in politics at all levels—federal, state, and local. If they succeed, they will still vote scoundrels into office, politics being what it is, but they will also elect Jeffersonian constitutionalists like Congressman Ron Paul, which would be our only chance to restore a domestic policy based on limited, decentralized government that does not crush prosperity, and a foreign policy that defends America, period.

THE TRUE HISTORY OF AMERICA

It is also high time that Americans stopped believing in the fantastic myths about the American founding that were invented by Alexander Hamilton, Daniel Webster, Joseph Story, and Abraham Lincoln, "proven" at gunpoint during the War between the States, and solidified in the minds of Americans by generations of public school propaganda.

The story of Jeffersonian federalism is the true history of America. The union was created by a voluntary compact of the states, and peaceful secession was always considered to be an essential part of any genuinely federal compact. It is a prerequisite for a self-governing people. Either the people are sovereign over their government or they are not. And if they are not, they are mere serfs, serving at the pleasure of their tax-collecting lords.[4]

In the early years of the American republic the mere threat of secession could discipline the national government and temper its proclivity to search for unconstitutional "implied powers" in the written Constitution. No one seriously challenged the New England Federalists when, after Jefferson's election in 1800, they plotted to secede for more than a decade. Nor was war threatened on New England when abolitionists such as William Lloyd Garrison advocated New England's secession from the southern states. America was founded by a war of secession from the British Empire, and nothing is more a part of the American political tradition.

The Hamilton/Webster/Lincoln superstitions about the holy and "mystical" perpetual union need to be exposed as the dangerous falsehoods that they are if sovereignty is ever to be returned to the American people. It is demonstrably untrue that state sovereignty never existed, that Madison never advanced the idea of "dual sovereignty" or federalism as the principal idea of the Constitution, that monopolistic government is a good thing, that "the whole people" of the United States adopted the Constitution in a national election, that secession is inherently evil, and that the federal government somehow created the states as its own administrative units. These are the Hamiltonian myths upon which the American Leviathan State

lives. They were established not by the force of logic and argumenta-
tion but by the death of more than 600,000 Americans in the 1860s.
They are nevertheless false and must be recognized as such.

Not all Americans are ignorant of their own history. There
have been small political movements in recent years to reintroduce
the idea of secession as a legitimate political tool.[5] Staten Island
voters voiced a preference to separate from the government of New
York City. Numerous local jurisdictions have separated themselves
from nearby metropolitan governmental bureaucracies by incorpo-
rating themselves as distinct political entities. In Vermont, the
"Second Vermont Republic" is a growing political movement to
have the state secede from the union and form its own country
(once again).[6] The Middlebury Institute for the Study of Separation, Secession, and Self-Determination was established to con-
duct research and educate the public on the issue.[7]

The Middlebury Institute's Web site includes information
about organized secession movements in South Carolina (naturally), Texas, Hawaii, Alaska, Vermont, California, Michigan, and
New Hampshire. An Internet poll taken on the Daily Kos Web
site found that 65 percent of the respondents were in favor of the
idea of peaceful secession.

UNDOING THE REVOLUTION OF 1913

Another step in ridding America of the curse of Hamiltonian centralization would be to repeal the Seventeenth Amendment and
return to the system the founders established for selecting U.S.
senators—that is, to have state legislatures appoint them. This
would not eliminate corruption, but it would reduce it and provide

a powerful incentive for senators to pay more attention to the people they purportedly represent and less attention to Washington, D.C., lobbyists.

Repealing the Sixteenth Amendment would also help roll back power from the federal government, since this amendment, which established the federal income tax, was the final nail in the coffin of federalism in America. Ending income taxation and replacing it with nothing—no national sales tax or "consumption tax" of any sort—would create the largest burst of prosperity in American history and finally put Washingtonians in their proper place as the mere custodians of a much smaller governmental bureaucracy and not the puppet masters of the entire world. It would also go a long way toward restoring citizen sovereignty and true federalism in America.

Lest you think abolishing the income tax and replacing it with nothing would be too radical a move, consider that if this step were taken in 2008, federal revenues would have been at about the same level they were in *1997*.[8] That's hardly a huge jump back, especially when you consider that in 1997 the government was already orders of magnitude larger than what is constitutionally legitimate. The abolition of the income tax and the IRS should therefore be viewed as only a modest first step in returning America to its constitutional roots.

"WIZARD OF OZ" ECONOMICS

For decades—especially since the 1930s—conservatives have preached strict constructionism when it comes to the Constitution. But all the preaching has been futile, for the simple reason that the federal government cannot be trusted to enforce limits on its own powers. The Jeffersonians understood this (as did the Hamiltonians, for that matter).

Only after the policies outlined above have given citizens of the states back their voice on constitutional matters will it make sense to attempt to enforce the enumerated powers of the Constitution. But once this rollback is achieved, it will be possible to bring back the Constitution of the founders and defeat the "living Constitution" of the neo-Hamiltonian nationalists.

It would be appropriate to amend the Constitution to prohibit the expenditure of any tax dollars on corporations, to outlaw protectionist tariffs, and to abolish the General Welfare Clause, all of which have caused so much mischief. These prohibitions were in fact achieved in the Confederate Constitution of 1861.[9] That is why the British historian of liberty Lord Acton, in corresponding with Robert E. Lee after the war, expressed his sadness over the demise of the Confederate Constitution; he saw it—and the right of secession—as the last best hopes of imposing restraints on "the sovereign power."[10] Nor was the Confederate Constitution unique. State governments included such restrictions in their own constitutions in the antebellum period, and they worked well.[11] The Hamiltonian destruction of constitutions by word-twisting lawyer/bureaucrats had not yet come to dominate law and politics in America.

The government's Hamiltonian monopoly on money must also be dismantled if the endless boom-and-bust cycles and the relentless decline in the value of a dollar are ever to be ended. For as Murray Rothbard wrote:

> [M]oney, in any market economy . . . is the nerve center of the economic system. If, therefore, the state is able to

gain unquestioned control over the unit of all accounts, the state will then be in a position to dominate the entire economic system, and the whole society. It will also be able to add quietly and effectively to its own wealth and to the wealth of its favorite groups, and without incurring the wrath that taxes often invoke. The state has understood this lesson since the kings of old began repeatedly to debase the coinage.[12]

Hamilton and his followers certainly understood this; that is why they battled for decades for governmental control of the money supply.

The most radical—and potentially beneficial—proposal for separating money and state has come from Austrian School economists like Rothbard who advocate an end to so-called fractional reserve banking. This is the system supervised by the Federal Reserve, whereby banks are permitted to lend far in excess of the amount of currency they have in their vaults. The Fed instructs them as to what percentage of their loans must be kept in reserve (the "reserve requirement"). By manipulating this reserve requirement the government can alter the amount of money in circulation. Instead, banks should be required to hold 100 percent reserves, backed by warehoused gold, the universally recognized money.

One reason to favor putting an end to fractional reserve banking is that it constitutes legalized fraud, as Rothbard explained:

> The banks began with 100 percent reserves, but then they shrewdly and keenly saw that only a certain proportion of

these demand liabilities were likely to be redeemed, so that it seemed safe either to lend out the gold for profit or to issue pseudo-warehouse receipts . . . for the gold, and to lend out those. The banks here take on the character of shrewd entrepreneurs. But so is an embezzler shrewd when he takes money out of the company till to invest in some ventures of his own. . . . The embezzler knows . . . that the auditor will come on June 1 to inspect the accounts; and he fully intends to repay the "loan" before then . . . a theft has occurred, and that theft should be prosecuted and not condoned.[13]

The other reason to end fractional reserve banking and replace it with 100 percent reserves backed by gold is that it would put an end to central bankers' political manipulation of the nation's money supply, and of society as a whole. As a side benefit, it would also puncture the myth—widely accepted among Americans—that central bankers are "Wizard of Oz"–type characters who can pull levers, push buttons, and pull cranks to "run the economy." Far from being omniscient, central bankers create inflation and boom-and-bust cycles, monopolize banking markets, and redistribute income surreptitiously. Yet they take credit for anything and everything that goes right in the economy.

Your author is not the first to note the similarity between central bankers and the Wizard of Oz. L. Frank Baum's book *The Wonderful Wizard of Oz*, on which the famous movie was based, was a commentary on the growing monetary problems of the late nineteenth century that were created by centralized banking. As the economists Mark Thornton and Robert B. Ekelund explain:

The Emerald (green) City is Washington and the Wizard of Oz (ounce of gold) is the president, who manipulates the population on behalf of the big-city banks. The Tin Man, Scarecrow, and Munchkins represent different groups of people while the Cowardly Lion represents William Jennings Bryan [an opponent of the gold standard] and Dorothy stands for "everyman," the average, good natured citizen, who does not have a clue about the underlying causes of the problems of society. The Yellow Brick Road is the gold standard. . . . Baum's story parallels the American banking system where the government and big banks controlled the economy in support of the industrial and financial interests in the East to the detriment of farmers, labor, and rural America, especially in the South and West.[14]

Baum's book was written after only about three decades of nationalized banking; the creation of the Fed in 1913 produced a system even more centralized than the one the Lincoln administration had created.

THE BEST HOPE

Hamilton's defenders are fond of pointing to a few good things the federal government has done while ignoring all of the bad. Many of the bad things were the work of the federal government in the first place. It was the federal government, for example, that helped enforce slavery with its Fugitive Slave Laws. It was the federal government that caused the Great Depression and, once it had begun, made it worse with even more counterproductive, interventionist economic policies. Hundreds of additional examples could be cited.

Hamilton's defenders also tend to ignore the fact that whatever good things the federal government has done could have been achieved either by state and local governments or by private individuals and charitable groups instead. It is difficult for many Americans to imagine that such alternative courses of action exist, since the federal government has so often stepped in and monopolized everything. But the truth is that everything from crime to poverty to discrimination might have been better handled by nonfederal programs. As a case in point, just look at the abysmal failure of the federal government's decades-long, exorbitantly expensive "War on Poverty." The problem is not just the ineffectiveness of the federal government's programs but also that its monopolizing proclivities crowd out private, localized efforts. Federal monopolization of poverty programs, for instance, sends the message that individuals need to do less to help their own neighbors in need. Social Security sends the message that we don't need to prepare as much for the care of our own elderly parents and grandparents; the state will take care of them. Public schools condition parents into believing that they don't need to make much of an effort to educate their own children; the state will take care of that. And on and on.

The only way to end the Hamiltonian curse of centralized, monopoly government is for Americans to once again embrace the Jeffersonian philosophy of government—to recognize that that government is best which governs least; that the citizens of the free and independent states are sovereign; and that they, along with their state and local representatives, are the best hope for the protection of liberty against the despotic proclivities of the central state.

Alexander Hamilton ended up beating out his rival Thomas Jefferson in the effort to shape the American government and its influence in citizens' lives. Because Hamilton won, the American people have lost.

NOTES

~

INTRODUCTION

1. Richard M. Weaver, *Ideas Have Consequences* (Chicago: University of Chicago Press, 1984).
2. Richard B. Morris, ed., *The Basic Ideas of Alexander Hamilton* (New York: Washington Square Press, 1956).
3. David N. Mayer, *The Constitutional Thought of Thomas Jefferson* (Charlottesville: University of Virginia Press, 1994), p. 188.
4. George F. Will, *Restoration: Congress, Term Limits, and the Recovery of Deliberative Democracy* (New York: Free Press, 1992), p. 167.
5. The title *Hamilton's Curse* is partly a response to a very well-written and well-argued book by John Steele Gordon entitled *Hamilton's Blessing*, about Hamilton's promotion of the national debt. See John Steele Gordon, *Hamilton's Blessing: The Extraordinary Life and Times of Our National Debt* (New York: Penguin, 1997). *Hamilton's Curse* will explain not only why Gordon was dead wrong about the national debt but also why almost all of Hamilton's other ideas, from protectionist tariffs to central banking to the subversive rewriting of the Constitution by federal judges, have been bad for America.
6. David Brooks, "Creating Capitalism," *New York Times,* April 25, 2004.
7. Ron Chernow, *Alexander Hamilton* (New York: Penguin, 2004), p. 6.
8. See Brooks, "Creating Capitalism," and David Brooks, "Reviving the Hamilton Agenda," *New York Times,* June 8, 2007.
9. Forrest McDonald, *Alexander Hamilton: A Biography* (New York: Norton, 1979), p. 361.

10. Stephen F. Knott, *Alexander Hamilton and the Persistence of Myth* (Lawrence: University Press of Kansas, 2002), p. 230.

11. See www.brookings.edu/projects/hamiltonproject/About-Us.aspx.

12. William Kristol and David Brooks, "What Ails Conservatism," *Wall Street Journal*, September 15, 1997, p. 22.

13. "Newt's Universe," *Time*, December 1995, p. 86.

CHAPTER 1

1. Ron Chernow, *Alexander Hamilton* (New York: Penguin, 2004), p. 210. Also see Ira Berlin and Leslie M. Harris, eds., *Slavery in New York* (New York: New-York Historical Society, 2005); Anne Farrow, Joel Lang, and Jennifer Frank, *Complicity: How the North Promoted, Prolonged, and Profited from Slavery* (Hartford, Conn.: Hartford Courant Co., 2005).

2. Clinton Rossiter, *Alexander Hamilton and the Constitution* (New York: Harcourt Brace, 1964), p. 6.

3. Ron Chernow, *Alexander Hamilton* (New York: Penguin, 2004), pp. 210–218.

4. William Graham Sumner, *Alexander Hamilton* (New York: University Society, 1905), p. 105.

5. Rossiter, *Constitution*, pp. 27–28.

6. Clyde Wilson, "The Yankee Problem in American History," in Wilson, *Defending Dixie: Essays in Southern History and Culture* (Columbia, S.C.: Foundation for American Education, 2006), p. 198.

7. Ibid., pp. 136–37.

8. Ibid., p. 176.

9. Rossiter, *Constitution*, p. 188.

10. Ibid., p. 6.

11. Ibid., p. 163.

12. Sumner, *Hamilton*, p. 111.

13. Thomas Jefferson to Major John Cartwright, June 5, 1824, in

Merrill D. Peterson, ed., *Thomas Jefferson: Writings* (New York: Library of America, 1984), p. 1493.

14. John Taylor, *New Views of the Constitution of the United States* (1823; reprint, Union, N.J.: Lawbook Exchange, 2002), p. 26. Also see Kenneth W. Royce, *Hologram of Liberty: The Constitution's Shocking Alliance with Big Government* (Austin, Tex.: Javelin Press, 1997).

15. Ibid., p. 27.

16. Rossiter, *Constitution,* p. 169.

17. Taylor, *New Views,* pp. 27, 28.

18. Ibid., p. 29.

19. Referring to Yates's notes on the Constitutional Convention, Taylor pointed out in *New Views* that "the expression in the constitution, 'shall be the supreme law of the land,' is restricted by its limitations and reservation, and did not convey any species of supremacy to the governments, going beyond the powers delegated or those reserved" (p. 78).

20. Ibid., p. 45.

21. Ibid., p. 46.

22. Ibid.

23. Ibid., p. 32.

24. Richard B. Morris, ed., *The Basic Ideas of Alexander Hamilton* (New York: Washington Square Press, 1956), p. 223.

25. Ibid., p. 225.

26. As cited in Felix Morley, *Freedom and Federalism* (Indianapolis: Liberty Fund, 1981), p. 36.

27. Claes Ryn, *America the Virtuous: The Crisis of Democracy and the Quest for Empire* (New Brunswick, N.J.: Transaction, 2003), p. 72.

28. Ibid.

29. Morley, *Freedom,* p. 41.

30. Rossiter, *Constitution,* p. 144.

31. Cecelia Kenyon, "Alexander Hamilton: Rousseau of the Right," *Political Science Quarterly* 73 (1958), p. 161.

32. Rossiter, *Constitution,* p. 144.

33. Ibid., p. 147.

34. Ibid., p. 203.

35. John Taylor, *Tyranny Unmasked* (Indianapolis: Liberty Fund, 1992).

36. Rossiter, *Constitution,* p. 196.

37. Harold C. Syrett and Jacob E. Cooke, eds., *The Papers of Alexander Hamilton* (New York: 1961), 4:222.

38. Ibid., 4:77–79.

39. Rossiter, *Constitution,* p. 200.

40. Jacob E. Cooke, ed., *The Reports of Alexander Hamilton* (New York: Harper & Row, 1964), p. 86.

41. Rossiter, *Constitution,* p. 202.

42. W. B. Allen, ed., *George Washington: A Collection* (Indianapolis: Liberty Fund, 1980), p. 521.

43. Cooke, *Reports of Hamilton,* p. 86.

44. Ibid., p. 172.

45. Rossiter, *Constitution,* p. 204.

46. Ibid., p. 205.

47. Cooke, *Reports of Hamilton,* p. 107.

48. Thomas Jefferson to George Washington, September 9, 1792, in Peterson, *Jefferson,* p. 994.

49. Jefferson, first annual message to Congress, ibid., p. 505.

50. Jefferson to General Thaddeus Kosciusko, April 12, 1802, ibid., p. 1103.

51. William Hogeland, *The Whiskey Rebellion* (New York: Scribner, 2006), p. 189.

52. Ibid., p. 42.

53. Ibid., p. 45.

54. John C. Miller, *The Federalist Era: 1789–1801* (New York: Harper & Row, 1960), p. 249.

55. Ibid.

56. Claude G. Bowers, *Jefferson and Hamilton: The Struggle for Democracy in America* (Boston: Houghton Mifflin, 1925), p. 211.

57. Ibid., p. 256.

58. Ibid.

59. Ibid., p. 235.

60. Ibid., p. 240.

CHAPTER 2

1. John Steele Gordon, *Hamilton's Blessing: The Extraordinary Life and Times of Our National Debt* (New York: Penguin, 1997), p. 8.

2. Thomas Jefferson to John Wayles Eppes, June 24, 1813, in Merrill D. Peterson, ed., *Thomas Jefferson: Writings* (New York: Library of America, 1984), p. 1282.

3. Ibid., p. 1280.

4. William Graham Sumner, *Alexander Hamilton* (New York: University Society, 1905), p. 144.

5. Jacob E. Cooke, ed., *The Reports of Alexander Hamilton* (New York: Harper & Row, 1964).

6. Gordon, *Blessing,* p. 25.

7. Claude G. Bowers, *Jefferson and Hamilton: The Struggle for Democracy in America* (Boston: Houghton Mifflin, 1925), p. 47.

8. Ibid.

9. Ibid., p. 48.

10. Ibid.

11. Ibid., p. 50.

12. Ibid.

13. Sumner, *Hamilton,* p. 149.

14. Paul Craig Roberts, "My Time with Supply-Side Economics," *Independent Review* 7, no. 3 (Winter 2003), pp. 393–97.

15. Saul Cornell, *The Other Founders: Anti-Federalism and the Dissenting*

Tradition in America, 1788–1828 (Chapel Hill: University of North Carolina Press, 1999).

16. Bowers, *Jefferson*, p. 54.

17. Ibid., p. 56.

18. Sumner, *Hamilton*, pp. 180, 150.

19. Ibid., p. 156.

20. Douglass Adair, ed., *The Federalist Papers* (New York: Penguin, 1980), pp. 171–72.

21. Bowers, *Jefferson*, p. 70.

22. Cornell, *Other Founders*, p. 179.

23. Ibid., p. 72.

24. Ibid., pp. 177–78.

25. Ibid., p. 177.

26. Gordon, *Blessing*, p. 29.

27. John C. Miller, *The Federalist Era: 1789–1801* (New York: Harper & Row, 1960), p. 53.

28. Ibid.

29. Bowers, *Jefferson*, p. 389.

30. Ibid., p. 404.

31. William J. Watkins Jr., *Reclaiming the American Revolution: The Kentucky and Virginia Resolutions and Their Legacy* (New York: Palgrave MacMillan, 2004).

32. The following information on the history of government debt is from Davis Dewey, *The Financial History of the United States* (New York: Elibron Classics, 2001).

33. Cited in Gordon, *Blessing*, p. 61.

34. Thomas DiLorenzo, *How Capitalism Saved America: The Untold History of Our Country, From the Pilgrims to the Present* (New York: Crown Forum, 2004).

35. Hans-Hermann Hoppe, *Democracy: The God That Failed* (New Brunswick, N.J.: Transaction, 2001), p. 27.

36. James M. Buchanan and Richard E. Wagner, *Democracy in Deficit: The Political Legacy of Lord Keynes* (New York: Academic Press, 1977), pp. 33–34.

37. Ibid., p. 49.

38. Bill Bonner and Addison Wiggin, *Empire of Debt: The Rise of an Epic Financial Crisis* (New York: Wiley, 2006).

CHAPTER 3

1. Alexander Hamilton, "Opinion on the Constitutionality of the Bank, February 23, 1791," in Jacob E. Cooke, ed., *The Reports of Alexander Hamilton* (New York: Harper & Row, 1964), pp. 83–114.

2. Ibid., p. xvii.

3. David N. Mayer, *The Constitutional Thought of Thomas Jefferson* (Charlottesville: University of Virginia Press, 1994), p. 191.

4. Cooke, *Reports of Hamilton*, p. 90.

5. Ibid.

6. Ibid., p. 86.

7. Murray N. Rothbard, *A History of Money and Banking in the United States: The Colonial Era to World War II* (Auburn, Ala.: Mises Institute, 2002), p. 69.

8. James J. Kilpatrick, *The Sovereign States* (Chicago: Regnery, 1957), p. 145.

9. Ibid.

10. The following account of the states' revolt against the BUS is from Kilpatrick, *Sovereign States*.

11. Ibid., p. 151.

12. Ibid.

13. Ibid., p. 152.

14. Ibid.

15. Richard Timberlake, *Monetary Policy in the United States: An*

Intellectual and Institutional History (Chicago: University of Chicago Press, 1993), p. 10.

16. Robert V. Remini, *Andrew Jackson and the Bank War* (New York: Norton, 1967), p. 36.

17. Rothbard, *History,* p. 76.

18. Murray Rothbard, *The Panic of 1819* (Auburn, Ala.: Mises Institute, 2007), p. 11.

19. Ibid., p 17.

20. Ibid.

21. Ibid., p. 19.

22. Ibid., p. 24.

23. Remini, *Jackson,* p. 39.

24. Ibid., p. 32.

25. Ibid., p. 15.

26. Rothbard, *History,* p. 91.

27. Remini, *Jackson,* p. 39.

28. Ibid.

29. Ibid., p 44.

30. Ibid., pp. 34–35.

31. Ibid., p. 35.

32. Ibid., p. 82.

33. Ibid., p. 83.

34. Murray Rothbard, *What Has Government Done to Our Money?* (Auburn, Ala.: Mises Institute, 2005), p. 66.

35. Murray Rothbard, *America's Great Depression* (Princeton, N.J.: D. Van Nostrand, 1963).

CHAPTER 4

1. Ron Chernow, *Alexander Hamilton* (New York: Penguin, 2004), p. 648.

2. John Taylor, *Tyranny Unmasked* (Indianapolis: Liberty Fund, 1992), p. 199.

3. St. George Tucker, *View of the Constitution of the United States* (Indianapolis: Liberty Fund, 1999), p. 27.

4. A concise discussion of the essence of *Marbury v. Madison* is found in Andrew Napolitano, *The Constitution in Exile* (Nashville, Tenn.: Thomas Nelson, 2006), pp. 28–35.

5. Ibid., p. 34.

6. Ibid., p. 35.

7. Ibid.

8. Thomas Jefferson to Judge Spencer Roane, September 6, 1819, in Merrill D. Peterson, ed., *Thomas Jefferson: Writings* (New York: Library of America, 1984), pp. 1426–27.

9. Woodrow Wilson, *Constitutional Government in the United States* (New Brunswick, N.J.: Transaction, 2001), p. 178.

10. Kevin R. C. Gutzman, *The Politically Incorrect Guide to the Constitution* (Washington, D.C.: Regnery, 2007), p. 83.

11. John Taylor, *New Views of the Constitution of the United States* (Union, N.J.: Lawbook Exchange, 2002), pp. 35–36.

12. Gutzman, *Guide,* pp. 82–85; Edward S. Corwin, *John Marshall and the Constitution* (New Haven, Conn.: Yale University Press, 1919), pp. 151–54.

13. Corwin, *Marshall,* pp. 177–82.

14. Gutzman, *Guide,* p. 86.

15. Edward S. Corwin, *The Commerce Power Versus States Rights* (Gloucester, Mass.: Peter Smith, 1962), p. 216.

16. Corwin, *Marshall,* p. 131.

17. Napolitano, *Exile,* p. 49.

18. Ibid., p. 49.

19. Gutzman, *Guide,* p. 92.

20. Corwin, *Marshall,* p. 182.

21. Ibid., p. 126.

22. Ibid., p. 173.

23. Ibid., p. 181.

24. Peterson, *Jefferson,* p. 1446.

25. Ibid.

26. Ibid.

27. Ibid.

28. Gutzman, *Guide,* p. 98.

29. Clinton Rossiter, *Alexander Hamilton and the Constitution* (New York: Harcourt Brace, 1964), p. 237.

30. Ibid.

31. Ibid.

32. Ibid., p. 244.

33. Ibid.

34. Ibid.

35. Ibid., p. 245.

36. Ibid.

37. Ibid., p. 246.

38. Ibid., p. 248.

39. Ibid.

40. Ibid., p. 249.

41. Napolitano, *Exile,* p. 133.

42. Hundreds of scholarly studies in the University of Chicago's *Journal of Law and Economics* have found, over and over again, that regulation rarely produces benefits but always entails heavy costs on society.

43. Frédéric Bastiat, *The Law* (1850; reprint, Auburn, Ala.: Mises Institute, 2007).

44. Bernard H. Siegan, *Economic Liberties and the Constitution,* 2nd ed. (New Brunswick, N.J.: Transaction, 2006), p. 182.

45. Napolitano, *Exile,* p. 140.

46. Ibid., p. 147.

CHAPTER 5

1. William Graham Sumner, *Alexander Hamilton* (New York: University Society, 1905), p. 176.

2. Ibid., p. 178.

3. Alexander Hamilton, *Report on Manufactures,* quoted in Peter McNamara, *Political Economy and Statesmanship: Smith, Hamilton, and the Foundation of the Commercial Republic* (DeKalb: Northern Illinois University Press, 1998), p. 135.

4. Sumner, *Hamilton,* p. 174.

5. Hamilton, *Report on Manufactures,* p. 10.

6. Nathan Rosenberg and L. E. Birdzell Jr., *How the West Grew Rich: The Economic Transformation of the Western World* (New York: Basic Books, 1986), p. 147.

7. Larry Schweikart, *The Entrepreneurial Adventure* (New York: Harcourt Brace, 2000), p. 38.

8. Jeremy Atack and Peter Passell, *A New Economic View of American History* (New York: Norton, 1994), p. 50.

9. Hamilton, *Report on Manufactures,* p. 141.

10. Ludwig von Mises, *Human Action: A Treatise on Economics* (Auburn, Ala.: Mises Institute, 1998), p. 270.

11. Hamilton, *Report on Manufactures,* p. 12.

12. Ibid.

13. Ibid., p. 118.

14. Sumner, *Hamilton,* p. 175.

15. Jacob E. Cooke, ed., *The Reports of Alexander Hamilton* (New York: Harper & Row, 1964), p. 167.

16. Hamilton, *Report on Manufactures,* p. 167.

17. Ibid.

18. Ibid., p. 168.

19. Ibid.

20. Ibid., p. 170.

21. Ibid., p. 171.

22. Ibid., p. 173.

23. Daniel Klein, "The Voluntary Provision of Public Goods? The Turnpike Companies of Early America," *Economic Inquiry,* October 1990, pp. 788–812.

24. Ibid.

25. Cooke, *Reports of Hamilton,* p. 204.

26. William Herndon and Jesse Weik, *Life of Lincoln* (New York: Da Capo, 1983), p. 161.

27. Ibid.

28. John Bach McMaster, *A History of the People of the United States* (New York: D. Appleton & Co., 1914), 6:628.

29. Sumner, *Hamilton,* p. 175.

30. David N. Mayer, *The Constitutional Thought of Thomas Jefferson* (Charlottesville: University of Virginia Press, 1994), p. 110.

31. Ibid.

32. Ibid.

33. Sumner, *Hamilton,* p. 175.

34. Maurice Baxter, *Henry Clay and the American System* (Lexington: University of Kentucky Press, 1995), p. 27. Also see "The American System" at http://en.wikipedia.org/wiki/American_System_(economic_plan).

35. Baxter, *Clay,* p. 6.

36. Ibid., p. 3.

37. Ibid., p. 27.

38. Ibid., p. 21.

39. Ibid., p. 26.

40. Ibid., p. 17.

41. Ibid., p. 27.

42. Chauncey Boucher, *The Nullification Controversy in South Carolina* (New York: Russell & Russell, 1968), p. 5.

43. Ibid.

44. Edgar Lee Masters, *Lincoln, the Man* (Columbia, S.C.: Foundation for Economic Education, 1997), p. 27.

45. Oliver Chitwood, *John Tyler: Champion of the Old South* (New York: Russell & Russell, 1964), pp. 226–29.

CHAPTER 6

1. Clinton Rossiter, *Alexander Hamilton and the Constitution* (New York: Harcourt Brace, 1964), p. 244.

2. Joseph Story, *Commentaries on the Constitution* (Durham, N.C.: Carolina Academic Press, 1995).

3. Jeffrey Hummel, *Emancipating Slaves, Enslaving Free Men* (Chicago: Open Court, 1996); Richard Timberlake, *Monetary History of the United States: An Intellectual and Institutional History* (Chicago: University of Chicago Press, 1993).

4. John Lamberton Harper, *American Machiavelli: Alexander Hamilton and the Origins of U.S. Foreign Policy* (New York: Cambridge University Press, 2004), p. 273.

5. Leonard P. Curry, *Blueprint for Modern America: Nonmilitary Legislation of the First Civil War Congress* (Nashville, Tenn.: Vanderbilt University Press, 1968), p. 116.

6. Heather Cox Richardson, *The Greatest Nation on the Earth: Republican Economic Policies During the Civil War* (Cambridge, Mass.: Harvard University Press, 1997), p. 72.

7. Ibid., p. 76.

8. Ibid., p. 87.

9. Ibid., p. 91.

10. Ibid.

11. Ibid.

12. Ibid., p. 94.

13. Mark Thornton and Robert B. Ekelund Jr., *Tariffs, Blockades, and Inflation: The Economics of the Civil War* (Wilmington, Del.: SR Books, 2004), p. 68.

14. Ibid.

15. Wesley Clair Mitchell, *A History of the Greenbacks, With Special Reference to the Economic Consequences of Their Issue, 1862–1865* (Chicago: University of Chicago Press, 1903).

16. Michael D. Bordo, Peter Rappoport, and Anna J. Schwartz, "Money versus Credit Rationing: Evidence for the National Banking Era, 1880–1914," in Claudia Goldin, ed., *Strategic Factors in Nineteenth-Century American Economic Growth* (Chicago: University of Chicago Press, 1992), pp. 189–223.

17. Curry, *Blueprint,* p. 150.

18. Frank L. Klement, *Lincoln's Critics: The Copperheads of the North* (Shippensburg, Pa.: White Mane Books, 1999).

19. Richardson, *Greatest Nation,* p. 125.

20. Abraham Lincoln, "Fragments on the Tariff," in *Abraham Lincoln: Speeches and Writings, 1832–1858* (New York: Library of America), p. 156.

21. Richardson, *Greatest Nation,* p. 125.

22. Ibid.

23. Frank Taussig, *The Tariff History of the United States* (New York: Putnam, 1931).

24. Ibid., p. 104.

25. Ibid., p. 146.

26. Jeremy Atack and Peter Passell, *A New Economic View of American History* (New York: Norton, 1994).

27. Carter Goodrich, *Government Promotion of American Canals and Railroads, 1800–1890* (Westport, Conn.: Greenwood Press, 1960), p. 231.

28. Albro Martin, *James J. Hill and the Opening of the Northwest* (New York: Oxford University Press, 1976); Michael P. Malone, *James J.*

Hill: Empire Builder of the Northwest (Norman: University of Oklahoma Press, 1996).

29. John W. Starr Jr., *Lincoln and the Railroads* (Manchester, N.H.: Ayer Co., 1981), p. 152.

30. Ibid.

31. Dee Brown, *Hear that Lonesome Whistle Blow* (New York: Owl Books, 2001), p. 49.

32. Ibid., p. 76.

33. Curry, *Blueprint*, p. 134.

34. Paul Gates, "Federal Land Policy in the South, 1866–1888," *Journal of Southern History,* August 1940, pp. 303–30.

35. Curry, *Blueprint*, p. 148.

36. Ibid.

37. Edward Martin, "A Complete and Graphic Account of the Crédit Mobilier Investigation," online at http://cprr.org/Museum/Credit_Mobilier_1873.html.

38. Ibid., p. 7.

39. Gabriel Kolko, *The Triumph of Conservatism: A Reinterpretation of American History, 1900–1916* (New York: Free Press, 1963).

40. Ibid., p. 3.

41. Butler Shaffer, *In Restraint of Trade: The Business Campaign Against Competition, 1918–1938* (Lewisburg, Pa.: Bucknell University Press, 1997), pp. 14, 15.

42. Ibid., p. 4.

43. Harold Demsetz, ed., *Efficiency, Competition, and Policy* (Cambridge, Mass.: Blackwell, 1989), p. 78.

44. George T. Brown, *The Gas Light Company of Baltimore: A Study of Natural Monopoly* (Baltimore, Md.: Johns Hopkins University Press, 1936), p. 75.

45. Horace M. Gray, "The Passing of the Public Utility Concept," *Journal of Land and Public Utility Economics,* February 1940, p. 9.

46. Adam Thierer, "Unnatural Monopoly: Critical Moments in the Development of the Bell System Monopoly," *Cato Journal,* Fall 1994, pp. 267–85.

47. John T. Flynn, *The Roosevelt Myth* (New York: Devin-Adair, 1948), p. 44.

48. Ibid., p. 43.

49. James Ford Rhodes, *History of the United States from the Compromise of 1850 to the Final Restoration of Home Rule at the South in 1877* (New York: Macmillan, 1900), p. 441.

50. James G. Randall, *Constitutional Problems Under Lincoln* (Urbana: University of Illinois Press, 1964), p. 30.

51. Clinton Rossiter, *Constitutional Dictatorship* (New York: Harcourt Brace, 1948), p. 226.

52. For example, in a September 7, 2006, *Wall Street Journal* article titled "Lincoln and Bush," former House Speaker Newt Gingrich called for an escalation of the war in the Middle East (and elsewhere)— even if it meant invading Iran, Saudi Arabia, Lebanon, Syria, and North Korea; to justify his plan, Gingrich cited Lincoln's actions during the War between the States, during which the president called for "intensifying the war" and "bringing the full might of the industrial North to bear until the war was won." In her book *In Defense of Internment,* the columnist Michelle Malkin made a case for imprisoning Muslim Americans en masse, as was done to Japanese Americans during World War II, by citing Lincoln's disregard for civil liberties and his imprisonment of thousands of political dissenters. When *Insight* magazine in 2005 published an article that supported the idea of intimidating members of Congress who opposed the war in Iraq, it naturally pointed to Lincoln's deportation of Congressman Vallandigham as its "Exhibit A." When the Columbia University Civil War historian Eric Foner opposed the breakup of

the Soviet Union in a 1991 article in *The Nation* magazine, he titled the article "Lincoln's Lesson."

CHAPTER 7

1. Ralph A. Rossum, *Federalism, the Supreme Court, and the Seventeenth Amendment: The Irony of Constitutional Democracy* (Lanham, Md.: Lexington Books, 2001), p. 96.
2. Ibid.
3. Ibid.
4. Ibid., p. 104.
5. Ibid.
6. Ibid.
7. Ibid., p. 105.
8. Ibid.
9. Ibid.
10. Ibid., p. 108.
11. Ibid., p. 100.
12. Ibid.
13. Ibid., p. 103.
14. Ibid.
15. Ibid, p. 183.
16. This phenomenon is the subject of Robert Higgs, *Crisis and Leviathan: Critical Episodes in the Growth of American Government* (New York: Oxford University Press, 1987).
17. Todd J. Zywicki, "Beyond the Shell and Husk of History: The History of the Seventeenth Amendment and Its Implications for Current Reform Proposals," *Cleveland State Law Review* 45 (1997), p. 174.
18. Ibid.
19. Rossum, *Federalism*, p. 233.

20. Thomas Jefferson, "First Inaugural Address," in Merrill D. Peterson, ed., *Thomas Jefferson: Writings* (New York: Library of America, 1984), p. 494.
21. Murray Rothbard, *Man, Economy and State, and Power and Market* (Auburn, Ala.: Mises Institute, 2004), p. 1156.
22. U.S. Department of Treasury, "Fact Sheets: Taxes," online at www.ustreas.gov/education/fact-sheets/taxes/ustax.shtml.
23. Higgs, *Crisis*, p. 113.
24. Frank Chodorov, *The Income Tax: Root of All Evil* (Greenwich, Conn.: Devin-Adair Company, 1974), p. 46.
25. Ibid., p. 47.
26. Ibid., p. 48.
27. Federal Reserve Bank of Minneapolis, "A History of Central Banking in the United States," online at www.minneapolisfed.org/centralbankhistory/bank.cfm.
28. Michael Lind, *What Lincoln Believed* (New York: Doubleday, 2005), p. 237.
29. Murray N. Rothbard, *A History of Money and Banking in the United States: The Colonial Era to World War II* (Auburn, Ala.: Mises Institute, 2002), p. 187.
30. Ibid.
31. Ibid., p. 258.
32. Lind, *Lincoln*, p. 246.
33. Ibid., p. 215.
34. Ibid., p. 249.
35. Rothbard, *History*, p. 259.
36. Ibid., p. 220.
37. Ibid., p. 248.
38. Murray Rothbard, *America's Great Depression* (Auburn, Ala.: Mises Institute, 2000).

CHAPTER 8

1. Thomas E. Woods Jr. and Kevin R. C. Gutzman, *Who Killed the Constitution: The Fate of American Liberty from World War I to George W. Bush* (New York: Crown Forum, 2008), p. 7.

2. Jim Powell, *Wilson's War: How Woodrow Wilson's Great Blunder Led to Hitler, Lenin, Stalin, and World War II* (New York: Crown Forum, 2005).

3. Timothy P. Carney, *The Big Ripoff: How Big Business and Big Government Steal Your Money* (New York: Wiley, 2006).

4. Ibid., p. 3.

5. Ibid., pp. 50–51.

6. Thomas DiLorenzo, "Farmed Robbery," *Free Market*, June 2005, p. 1.

7. Ibid.

8. Carney, *Big Ripoff*, p. 61.

9. Peter Bauer, *The Development Frontier* (Cambridge, Mass.: Harvard University Press, 1991).

10. Chris Edwards, "Downsizing the Federal Government," Cato Institute Policy Analysis, June 2, 2004.

11. Steven Greenhut, *Abuse of Power: How the Government Misuses Eminent Domain* (Cabin John, Md.: Seen Locks Press, 2004).

12. William J. Quirk and Randall Bridwell, *Judicial Dictatorship* (New Brunswick, N.J.: Transaction, 1997).

13. Andrew Napolitano, *The Constitution in Exile* (Nashville, Tenn.: Thomas Nelson, 2006), p. 133.

14. Ibid., p. 134.

15. Kevin R. C. Gutzman, *The Politically Incorrect Guide to the Constitution* (Washington, D.C.: Regnery, 2007), p. 167.

16. Bernard H. Siegan, *Economic Liberties and the Constitution* (New Brunswick, N.J.: Transaction, 2006), p. 182.

17. Clinton Rossiter, *Alexander Hamilton and the Constitution* (New York: Harcourt Brace, 1964), p. 205.

18. Ibid.

19. "Thomas Jefferson on Interpreting the Constitution," online at http://etext.virginia.edu/jefferson/quotations/fef1020.htm.

20. Napolitano, *Exile,* p. 169.

21. Ibid., p. 178.

22. Ibid., p. 185.

23. Ibid., p. 188.

24. Gutzman, *Guide,* p. 172.

25. Gene Healy, "Against Libertarian Centralism," www.lewrockwell.com/healy/healy4.html.

26. George P. Fletcher, *Our Secret Constitution: How Lincoln Redefined American Democracy* (New York: Oxford University Press, 2001), p. 6.

27. Ibid., p. 5.

28. Ibid.

29. Ibid., pp. 8, 12.

30. See Thomas DiLorenzo, *Lincoln Unmasked: What You're Not Supposed to Know About Dishonest Abe* (New York: Crown Forum, 2006).

31. Clyde Wilson, "The American President: From Cincinnatus to Caesar," in John Denson, ed., *Reassessing the Presidency* (Auburn, Ala.: Mises Institute, 2001), p. 708.

32. Ibid.

33. Ibid.

34. Ibid., p. 709.

35. David Gelernter, *Americanism: The Fourth Great Western Religion* (New York: Doubleday, 2007).

36. Gene Healy and Timothy Lynch, *Power Surge: The Constitutional Record of George W. Bush* (Washington, D.C.: Cato Institute, 2007).

37. Robert Weintraub, "Congressional Supervision of Monetary Policy," *Journal of Monetary Economics,* April 1978, pp. 341–62.

38. Ibid.

39. James Bovard, "The IRS vs. You," *American Spectator,* November 1995; online at www.jimbovard.com/American%20Spectator%20 Nov%2095%20The%20IRS%20vs%20You.htm.

40. Ibid.

41. Ibid.

42. Michael Lind, *Hamilton's Republic* (New York: Free Press, 1997), p. 299.

43. "Over Half of Americans on the Dole," *Christian Science Monitor,* August 14, 2007, p. 1.

44. Charles Murray, *Losing Ground* (New York: Basic Books, 1984).

45. John Lamberton Harper, *American Machiavelli: Alexander Hamilton and the Origins of U.S. Foreign Policy* (New York: Cambridge University Press, 2004).

46. Joseph Stromberg, "The Role of State Monopoly Capitalism in the American Empire," *Journal of Libertarian Studies,* Summer 2001, pp. 57–93.

47. Ibid., p. 70.

48. Ibid., p. 78.

49. Ibid., p. 79.

50. Felix Morley, *Freedom and Federalism* (1959; reprint, Indianapolis: Liberty Fund, 1981), p. 126.

51. Ibid., p. 124.

52. Ibid., p. 125.

CONCLUSION

1. Michael Lind, *Hamilton's Republic* (New York: Free Press, 1997), p. xv.

2. Laurence J. Kotlikoff, "Generational Accounting," *NBER Reporter,* Winter 1995–96, pp. 8–14.

3. William J. Watkins Jr., *Reclaiming the American Revolution: The Kentucky and Virginia Resolutions and Their Legacy* (New York: Palgrave

Macmillan, 2004); James J. Kilpatrick, *The Sovereign States* (Chicago: Regnery, 1957).

4. See Thomas E. Woods Jr., *The Politically Incorrect Guide to American History* (Washington, D.C.: Regnery, 2005); and Kevin R. C. Gutzman, *The Politically Incorrect Guide to the Constitution* (Washington, D.C.: Regnery, 2007).

5. David Gordon, ed., *Secession, State and Liberty* (New Brunswick, N.J.: Transaction, 1998).

6. See www.secondvermontrepublic.org.

7. See www.middleburyinstitute.org.

8. The proposed 2008 federal budget was approximately $2.8 trillion, with $1.2 trillion in income tax revenue expected. Subtracting the latter number from the former leaves a budget of $1.6 trillion, which is where federal budget expenditures stood in 1997. See U.S. Bureau of the Census, online at www.census.gov/prod/2006pubs/07statab/fedgov.pdf.

9. Marshall DeRosa, *The Confederate Constitution of 1861: An Inquiry into American Constitutionalism* (Columbia: University of Missouri Press, 1991).

10. J. Rufus Fears, ed., *Selected Writings of Lord Acton*, vol. 1, *Essays in the History of Liberty* (Indianapolis: Liberty Fund, 1985), p. 363.

11. Carter Goodrich, *Government Promotion of American Canals and Railroads, 1800–1890* (Westport, Conn.: Greenwood Press, 1960).

12. Murray Rothbard, *What Has Government Done to Our Money?* (Auburn, Ala.: Mises Institute, 2005), p. 139.

13. Ibid., pp. 160–61.

14. Mark Thornton and Robert B. Ekelund Jr., *Tariffs, Blockades, and Inflation: The Economics of the Civil War* (Wilmington, Del.: SR Books, 2004), p. 78.

ACKNOWLEDGMENTS

I would like to thank my editor at Crown Forum, Jed Donahue, for his insightful comments that, as usual, have greatly improved the presentation of this book. Thanks also to my colleagues and associates at the Ludwig von Mises Institute, who have provided me with a sounding board for my ideas and writing. The Institute's resources and programs are indispensable to all of my research and writing, for which I would like to thank my good friends Lew Rockwell, president, and Jeff Tucker, vice president of research.

My three girls—Stacey, Rosie, and Molly—were extremely supportive and helpful, for which I am grateful.

—Thomas J. DiLorenzo

INDEX

ABOUT THE AUTHOR

~

THOMAS J. DILORENZO is the author of *The Real Lincoln, How Capitalism Saved America*, and *Lincoln Unmasked*. His work has appeared in *The Wall Street Journal, Barron's, Reader's Digest, USA Today*, and *National Review*, among other publications. A senior faculty member at the Ludwig von Mises Institute in Alabama and a professor of economics at Loyola College in Maryland, DiLorenzo resides near Baltimore.

Also by
Thomas J. DiLorenzo

The Real Lincoln
A New Look at Abraham Lincoln,
His Agenda, and an Unnecessary War
$15.95 paper ($22.95 Canada)
978-0-7615-2646-9

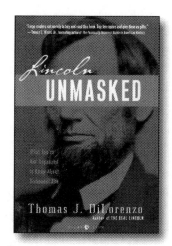

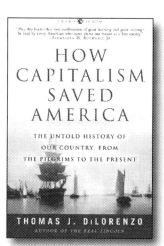

How Capitalism Saved America
The Untold History of Our Country,
from the Pilgrims to the Present
$14.95 paper ($21.00 Canada)
978-1-4000-8331-2

Lincoln Unmasked
What You're Not Supposed to Know
About Dishonest Abe
$12.95 paper ($16.95 Canada)
978-0-307-33842-6

Available from Three Rivers Press wherever books are sold.

Printed in the United States
by Baker & Taylor Publisher Services